Fremdsprachentexte

Fifty English Sonnets

Herausgegeben von
Michael Hanke

Philipp Reclam jun. Stuttgart

Diese Ausgabe darf nur in der Bundesrepublik Deutschland, in Österreich und in der Schweiz vertrieben werden.

Universal-Bibliothek Nr. 9085

Gesamtherstellung: Reclam, Ditzingen. Printed in Germany 2001
RECLAM und UNIVERSAL-BIBLIOTHEK sind eingetragene Marken der Philipp Reclam jun. GmbH & Co., Stuttgart
ISBN 3-15-009085-7

www.reclam.de

Einleitung

Die ersten Sonette entstanden im frühen 13. Jahrhundert, am Hof des Stauferkaisers Friedrich II. im sizilianischen Palermo. Verfasser waren universal gebildete Juristen und Staatsdiener, unter ihnen der erste Virtuose des Fachs, Friedrichs Notar und Kanzler Giacomo da Lentini. Der kunstbegeisterte Kaiser förderte die schriftstellerische Betätigung seiner Untergebenen mit Nachdruck. Er ließ sogar Dichterwettkämpfe veranstalten, bei denen die vom Minnekult der Trobadors inspirierte Lyrik vorgetragen und begeistert aufgenommen wurde. Weniger gut sind wir über die Genese des Sonetts informiert. Hugo Friedrich, einer der besten Kenner der italienischen Lyrik, folgt der Auffassung älterer Gelehrter, wenn er das Genre aus der einfachen Kanzonenstrophe – bestehend aus einem zweiteiligen Aufgesang und einem einteiligen, kürzeren Abgesang – hervorgehen lässt (Friedrich, S. 16 ff.).

Einen ersten Höhepunkt erreicht die Sonettkunst mit dem *Canzoniere* des Francesco Petrarca (1304–74). Die Wirkung seines Zyklus entfaltete sich wie ein Flächenbrand, wobei allerdings oft weniger Petrarca selbst als seine Nachfolger und Nachahmer das Vorbild abgaben. Zunächst in Italien, dann in Spanien, Portugal, Frankreich, England, schließlich in Deutschland gab es kaum einen Dichter von Rang, der nicht eine Hand voll Sonette schrieb, die als Klassiker des Genres Anerkennung fanden (Reichenberger, S. 885 ff.).

In England hätte die Geschichte des Sonetts Ende des 14. Jahrhunderts beginnen können, als Chaucer seinem Versroman *Troilus and Criseyde* die Übersetzung eines Petrarca-Sonetts einfügte (I,400–420: »Canticus Troili«). Doch gab er die Form des italienischen Originals zugunsten der speziell für den *Troilus* entworfenen siebenzeiligen Strophe des *rhyme royal* (Reimschema *ababbcc*) auf.

Der erste englische Sonettist heißt Thomas Wyatt (1503–1542) und begegnet uns am Hof Heinrichs VIII. In den meisten seiner Gedichte bedient er sich italienischer Vorlagen und behandelt im Einklang mit dem humanistischen Imitatio-Konzept das Thema Liebe in Form freier Nachahmung. Wyatt war Diplomat, der im Auftrag des Königs nach Italien reiste, sich vom dort grassierenden Sonettfieber der Petrarkisten anstecken ließ, die neue Form nach England brachte und sie seinem jungen Freund Henry Howard, Earl of Surrey, als verpflichtendes Erbe überließ. Er gilt mit Recht als Vater des Sonetts in England, Surrey als erster konsequenter Verfechter einer Formvariante, die von Shakespeare zur Vollendung geführt wurde und als englisches Sonett (*English sonnet*) oder Shakespeare-Sonett (*Shakespearean sonnet*) in die Literaturgeschichte eingegangen ist. Bevor wir uns jedoch dieser reformiert-insularen Variante zuwenden, werfen wir einen Blick auf die Formmerkmale des italienischen Originals, das auch als Petrarca-Sonett bezeichnet wird. Erst dadurch gewinnen wir einen Eindruck von den Schwierigkeiten, denen sich Wyatt gegenübersah, als er die Form in England heimisch zu machen versuchte.

Das italienische Sonett zeigt eine klare Zweiteilung in Oktett (bestehend aus zwei Quartetten) und Sextett (bestehend aus zwei Terzetten). Das Reimschema des Oktetts ist genau festgelegt (*abba abba*), das des Sextetts ist flexibler gehalten (*cde cde*, *cdc dcd* oder *cde dce*), wobei im Sextett die Verwendung von Paarreimen ausgeschlossen ist. Daraus ergibt sich die klangliche und syntaktische Zweiteilung, der eine gedankliche Wende oder Zäsur (ital. *volta*; engl. *turn*) zwischen den Zeilen 8 und 9 entspricht (Fuller, S. 1 ff.).

Der Aufbau eines Petrarca-Sonetts lässt sich an John Keats' »On First Looking into Chapman's Homer« (1816) demonstrieren, da hier die italienische Struktur, vor allem die kunstvolle Wende zwischen Oktett und Sextett, beibehalten wird. Im Oktett spricht Keats von einem wiederholten Erleben (»Much have I travelled«, »Oft […] had I been told«), im Sextett von einer einmaligen, sein ganzes bisheriges Leben verändernden Erfahrung. Zunächst hört er von Homer aus der Ferne, aus zweiter Hand, dann begegnet er ihm unmittelbar, in der kongenialen *Odyssee*-Übersetzung des Elisabethaners George Chapman. Die für das italienische Vorbild charakteristische Zweiteilung findet auch in der Bildlichkeit ihren Niederschlag: Im Oktett erscheinen nur Metaphern, im Sextett nur Vergleiche. Mit seinem Faible für konturenscharfe Bilder, fein ziselierte Perioden und rhythmische Eleganz hatte Keats keine Schwierigkeiten, die italienische Form in den Dienst der eigenen Aussage zu stellen (Viebrock, S. 83 ff.).

Eine solche Meisterleistung darf man vom Pionier Wyatt nicht erwarten, auch wenn er sich mit zahlreichen selbsterfundenen Strophenformen als einer der großen englischen Liebeslyriker erweist. Es ist absurd, wenn Funktionalisten noch heute versuchen, sich und anderen einzureden, Wyatts traurige Erfahrungen als Liebender seien für die ungehobelte metrische Oberfläche und den holprigen Gedankengang seiner Sonette verantwortlich. Selbst für den nicht bewiesenen Fall, dass er tatsächlich persönliche Erfahrungen behandelt und mit den Sprechern der Gedichte identifiziert werden darf, erklärt dies nicht, warum er seine Liebesklagen außerhalb der Sonettform so viel beredter vorträgt. Schließlich wird auch anderswo Liebesleid poetisch gestaltet – oft sogar mit Gusto, wie in Shakespeares 129. Sonett –, ohne dass der Dichter deswegen in abgründiges Stottern gerät. Die Lösung dürfte weniger in Wyatts seelischer Befindlichkeit als in dichtungstechnischen Gegebenheiten seiner Zeit zu suchen sein (Standop, S. 76 ff.).

Wyatts Probleme liegen vor allem in der Reimtechnik und der syntaktischen Struktur seiner Sextette klar zutage. Zu seiner Zeit waren in England zwar Quartette und Distichen (*couplets*) bekannt, nicht aber Terzette, und gerade im Umgang mit ihnen beweist er keine glückliche Hand.

Um Schwierigkeiten zu vermeiden, verwendet er in 27 seiner 32 Sonette im Sextett das Reimschema *cddcee* – eine experimentelle Sonderform, die Cino da Pistoia mit einigen wenigen Sonetten zur Zeit von Wyatts Aufenthalt in Italien bekannt gemacht hatte (Bullock). In »Who so list to hunt« setzt Wyatt an die Stelle von Oktett und Sextett drei Quartette und ein Distichon und versucht, seine Abweichung von der italienischen Form zu kaschieren. Vergebens: Form und Inhalt klaffen auseinander, die Prägnanz des Schlussreimpaares fordert syntaktische Selbständigkeit und lässt sich dem zweiten Terzett nicht zwanglos eingliedern. Wyatts Strukturprobleme entsprangen offenbar dem Versuch, sich in seinen Imitationen möglichst eng an sein Vorbild Petrarca anzulehnen.

Die englische Verssprache bot nach einer langen Zeit der metrischen Verwilderung noch keine Möglichkeit, der italienischen Kunst lyrischer Seelenchirurgie in einer metrisch-gedanklich kongenialen 1:1-Übertragung gerecht zu werden. Von den Höhen italienischer Sonettkunst besehen, musste Wyatts Versuch, unter Beibehaltung von Form und Thema eine ähnliche Geschlossenheit und Wirkung wie Petrarca und seine Nachfolger zu erzielen, geradezu vermessen erscheinen. Vergessen wir nicht, dass den Italienern eine Fülle von Reimwörtern zur Verfügung stand, von der ihre Kollegen jenseits des Kanals nur träumen konnten. Jeder Versuch, eine englische Übertragung gehaltlich und formal exakt im Kielwasser des Originals zu halten, war – vorerst jedenfalls – zum Scheitern verurteilt.

Es war der findige Surrey, der dem Sonett zu guter Letzt doch ein Heimatrecht in England verschaffte. Mit den Problemen des Freundes war er bestens vertraut, und beim Versuch, sie zu lösen, scheute er sich nicht, die notwendigen Konsequenzen zu ziehen. Surrey vereinfachte das Reimschema und gab damit die Beschränkung der Reimzahl und die Zweigliederung in Oktett und Sextett auf. Erst bei ihm finden wir die markante Gliederung in drei fortlaufend kreuzgereimte Quartette und Schlussreimpaar (*abab cdcd efef gg*).

Das Distichon gilt von nun an als Markenzeichen des englischen Sonetts, weil es einen dem Petrarca-Sonett wesensfremden Schlussakzent setzt. Es war prädestiniert für die knappe, je nach Bedarf ironisch, scherzhaft, epigrammatisch zugespitzte Summationsformel oder den pointierten Knalleffekt von Michael Draytons »Since there's no help« (publ. 1619), wo die Aussage der drei Quartette zum Schluss auf den Kopf gestellt wird. Mit diesem Kunstgriff lockerte Surrey die Regeln des italienischen Typus, weckte das englische Sonett aus seinem Dornröschenschlaf und schickte es auf eine bis heute nicht abgerissene Erfolgslaufbahn. Selbst das Desinteresse der Klassizisten im 18. Jahrhundert hat der Popularität des Genres nicht geschadet.

Surreys literaturgeschichtliche Bedeutung ist damit gesichert, seine dichterische Praxis allerdings eher enttäuschend. Er ist der Erste in einer langen Reihe von Dichtern, die lästige metrische Probleme dadurch beseitigen, dass sie holprige Stellen mit Füllwörtern wie *doth, eke, sweet* ausgießen, so dass sich der Respekt vor seiner oft gepriesenen Eleganz bald verflüchtigt. Metrische Glätte um jeden Preis: So lautete seine Devise. Doch selbst Shakespeare hat Surreys billige Tricks keineswegs verschmäht, wenn es darum ging, in kürzester Zeit einen rhythmisch fugenlosen Vers zu Papier zu bringen.

Unter dem Vorbild von Petrarca, Wyatt, Surrey war das zentrale Thema des Sonetts bis Shakespeare überwiegend, wenn nicht ausschließlich, die Liebe. Allein in den Jahren 1592–97 wurden in England etwa 2000 Liebessonette gedruckt, und selbst bei noch so reizvollen Abstechern in den Bereich des Religiösen, Ästhetischen und Politischen, mit denen etwa Sidney seinen Sonettzyklus *Astrophel and Stella* anreichert, lässt der Dichter die besungene Dame nicht aus dem Blick. Nirgends – nicht einmal in den möglicherweise biographisch motivierten Werken Wyatts –

sollte man von einer tatsächlich vorhandenen oder auch nur ernsthaft erstrebten Liebesbeziehung ausgehen. Wie in der Dichtung der Trobadors und der späteren Minnesänger handelt es sich um eine Kunstübung, motiviert durch die unüberbrückbare Distanz zwischen dem Mann und der sittlich und gesellschaftlich hoch über ihm stehenden Dame.

Um bei Sidney zu bleiben: Seine Stella, Penelope Devereux, Lady Rich, war längst verheiratet, als er sie zur Adressatin seines Zyklus erkor. Eine Liebesbeziehung, ein gesellschaftlich sanktioniertes Verhältnis gar, wäre kaum denkbar gewesen – es sei denn, die beiden hätten ein Vergnügen daran gehabt, sich im Hofklatsch zu sonnen. Abgesehen davon befand sich auch Sidney (zu seiner vollsten Zufriedenheit übrigens) in festen Händen. Die gebotene Distanz war da, der inspirierte Dichter konnte ans Werk gehen.

Vor solchem Hintergrund ist es einleuchtend, dass die Forschung diese Lyrik als Teil eines komplizierten, bis heute nicht restlos erforschten *game of love* versteht (Peterson). Bei diesem Spiel konnten sich die Autoren auf das bewährte Kompositionsprinzip der imitativen Konkurrenz berufen. Nicht nur die Epiker nach Homer haben versucht, ihre jeweiligen Vorläufer in einer Olympiade der Imitation und Neugestaltung zu übertreffen, sondern auch die Sonettisten: Sie schrieben für ein kunstverständiges Publikum, das mit dieser Tradition vertraut war.

Als Beispiel sei Shakespeares 130. Sonett genannt, die berühmte Huldigung an die geheimnisvolle *dark lady.* Hier geht es ihm keineswegs darum, den Motivbestand des Petrarkismus der Lächerlichkeit preiszugeben. Vielmehr spielt er mit ihm, um seiner neoplatonischen Entsinnlichung entgegenzuwirken. Und mit dieser Praxis ist er weder der Einzige noch der Erste. Schon Sidney hatte sich im Programmsonett von *Astrophel and Stella* (»Loving in truth«) mit den Grenzen und Möglichkeiten der traditionellen Panegyrik auseinandergesetzt. Shakespeare liefert nur eine von vielen möglichen Illustrationen zu Sidneys Gedanken.

Shakespeares Beitrag zur Erweiterung des Metaphernbestands ist – bei aller berechtigten Bewunderung für seinen selbständigen, geradezu selbstherrlichen Umgang mit der Tradition – oft überschätzt worden. Die für ihn reklamierten Bildbereiche des Handels, des Gerichts- und Kriegswesens, des Gewerbes und des Theaters lassen sich schon in der älteren Dichtung nachweisen. Doch ist er der Erste, der in seinen Sonetten den naturverbundenen Charakter der Liebe feiert und den Liebenden, wenngleich stilisiert und mit dem rhetorischen Aplomb des geborenen Dramatikers gerüstet, in seinen wenig erbaulichen Reflexionen nach dem Geschlechtsakt zeigt (Sonett 129).

Auf dem Gebiet des Sonetts ist Shakespeare der mit Abstand größte Formvirtuose, weil er bei unveränderter äußerer Struktur über eine Fülle von Stil- und Tonlagen verfügt. Bewundernswert, wie er im weit gespannten sprachlichen Bogen von Sonett 29 bei der Gestaltung des Selbstmitleids zielsicher bis an die Grenze zum Kitsch vorstößt (Z. 8), um dann das Sextett völlig unerwartet – psychologisch jedoch absolut plausibel – mit der sich gen Himmel erhebenden Lerche und dem seiner Depressionen ledigen Sprecher triumphal ausklingen lässt. Was Wyatt versagt bleibt, gelingt Shakespeare ein halbes Jahrhundert später mühelos: die Integration der italienischen *volta* ins englische Schema. Der Gedankengang des italienischen und die Form des englischen Sonetts durchdringen sich.

Auch Shakespeares größter Zeitgenosse John Donne ist lange als Antipetrarkist missverstanden worden. Man übersah, dass kritische Kontrafakturen sich zuvor schon in Italien großer Beliebtheit erfreut hatten. Donnes Genialität als Sonettist zeigt sich auf anderem Gebiet. Er machte Bild- und Motivfelder, die bislang für die Liebeslyrik reserviert waren, der religiösen Dichtung nutzbar. Dem profanen Charakter der blasphemischen Liebeslyrik des jungen *libertin* entspricht die gegenläufige Tendenz der religiösen Lyrik des sich abgeklärt wähnenden Dean of St Paul's. Hier sind es vor allem die *Holy Sonnets* (1609), in denen er Bilder seiner frühen Liebesdichtung in einen ebenso neuen wie blendend originellen Argumentationszusammenhang rückt und den Leser mit *conceits* – mit überraschenden, schockierenden, dennoch der Logik nicht entbehrenden Metaphern – zu neuen Einsichten zwingt. So etwa, wenn er im Sonett »Batter my heart« auf die uralte Metapher von der Liebe als Kampf zurückgreift, um die alles irdische Maß sprengende, scheinbar als reine Zerstörung sich manifestierende Allmacht der Liebe Gottes zu demonstrieren. Das Gedicht mündet in die Paradoxie, Gott möge den Sprecher – dem die Rolle der vom Teufel umworbenen Frau zufällt – vergewaltigen. Nur in der Vereinigung mit Gott findet der Mensch die zur Erlangung ewigen Heils erforderliche Keuschheit.

Nur selten vermochte ein englischer Dichter geistig-seelische Vorgänge auf so drastische und zugleich einleuchtende Weise begreiflich zu machen wie Donne. Mit den *Holy Sonnets* und dem älteren Zyklus *La Corona* (1607) ist er – sieht man von seinem weniger wortgewaltigen Zeitgenossen Drummond of Hawthornden ab – der Stifter des religiösen Sonetts in England. Von nun an stehen religiöse Themen und Motive immer wieder im Zentrum der Sonettdichter: von George Herbert über Christina Rossetti, Hopkins und Alice Meynell bis zu Charles Causley.

Der nächste große Sonettist ist John Milton, und auch er setzt neue Akzente. Abgesehen davon, dass er die italienische Grundform der englischen Filiation gleichberechtigt an die Seite stellt, nimmt er dezidierter als irgendeiner seiner Vorläufer das Sonett für die Behandlung öffentlicher und persönlicher Konflikte in Anspruch. Dabei ist seine Gedankenführung nicht immer leicht zu durchschauen. Indiz dafür ist die in der englischen Sonettdichtung bis dahin einmalig komplizierte Syntax. Zudem überspielt Milton bewusst die Grenzen zwischen Quartetten und Terzetten (bzw. Oktett und Sextett), was vor ihm nur Herbert – allerdings viel zurückhaltender – getan hatte. Es gefällt dem großen Epiker, auch das vergleichsweise fragile Gefäß des Sonetts bis zum Bersten anzufüllen. In seinen schwächeren Momenten führt das allerdings zu Manierismen, die Dr. Johnson zu dem Ausspruch veranlasst haben: »Milton was a genius that could cut a Colossus from a rock, but could not carve heads upon cherry-stones« (Boswell, S. 320). Zweifellos hat Miltons überragende Gestalt die Leistungen der unmittelbar folgenden Generationen in den Schatten gestellt und den Spielraum für formale und inhaltliche Neuerungen empfindlich eingeschränkt. Andererseits hat er, nicht zuletzt durch seinen Rückgriff auf die petrarkische Urform, wesentlich zur späteren Erneuerung des Sonetts gegen Ende des 18. Jahrhunderts beigetragen.

Wordsworths »Milton! thou shouldst be living at this hour« (1802) ist nicht nur nostalgisch-bewundernder Blick auf vergangene Größe, es ist zugleich das erste von zahllosen bedeutenden englischen Dichtersonetten von Keats über die Viktorianer bis zu Campbell und Auden. In Milton fanden die Romantiker ihr legitimierendes Vorbild für eine Sonettform, die elastisch genug war, sich jeder Gedanken- und Gefühlsregung des intuitionsgeleiteten Künstlers anzupassen, ohne ihn über die traditionelle 14-Zeiligkeit hinaus auf ein formales Muster festzulegen. Wie heißt es in einem experimentellen Sonett von Keats aus dem Jahr 1819?

> If by dull rhymes our English must be chained,
> And, like Andromeda, the Sonnet sweet
> Fettered, in spite of painèd loveliness,
> Let us find out, if we must be constrained,
> Sandals more interwoven and complete
> To fit the naked foot of Poesy:
> Let us inspect the lyre, and weigh the stress

Of every chord, and see what may be gained
By ear industrious, and attention meet;
Misers of sound and syllable, no less
Than Midas of his coinage, let us be
Jealous of dead leaves in the bay wreath crown;
So, if we may not let the Muse be free,
She will be bound with garlands of her own.

Das Sonett schafft sich aus eigener Kraft, unabhängig von den Spielregeln Petrarcas und Shakespeares, die seiner spezifischen Aussage gemäße Form. Paradoxerweise zeigt sich aber in den zitierten Versen doch auch etwas vom Zwang, den eine übermächtige Tradition nach wie vor auszuüben vermag: Keats' Absichtserklärung ist von apologetischen Untertönen nicht frei. Die Elisabethaner waren da ungezwungener. Schon zu Shakespeares Zeiten gab es Sonette mit sechzehn Zeilen und reimlose Sonette, ohne dass die Autoren auch nur ein Wort darüber verloren hätten. Keats selbst folgte, wie wir am Beispiel des Chapman-Homer-Sonetts gesehen haben, zunächst dem petrarkischen Sonett-Typus, griff allerdings später – von einigen Experimenten abgesehen – auf das shakespearesche Muster zurück.

Die Viktorianer Christina Rossetti und Gerard Manley Hopkins sind die bedeutendsten religiösen Dichter des 19. Jahrhunderts. Doch abgesehen von ihrem gemeinsamen Thema verbindet die beiden wenig miteinander. Christina Rossetti schreibt eine glasklare Lyrik, melancholisch grundiert, für deren Verständnis selbst ein deutscher Leser kaum je zum Wörterbuch greifen muss. Hopkins dagegen ist ein außerordentlich schwieriger Dichter, der in seiner Freude am metrischen Experiment, mit seinen Neologismen, Archaismen und seinem das Manieristische streifenden Hang zur Dunkelheit ein konzentriertes Lesen erfordert. Er ist ein *poet's poet,* der stärker als jeder andere Dichter seiner Zeit ins 20. Jahrhundert hineingewirkt hat.

Yeats, Pound und Eliot, die drei Großen der modernen Lyrik, haben dem Sonett wenig abgewinnen können. Yeats zog die Stanzenform vor und schrieb nur zwei, dafür aber herausragende mythologische Sonette (»Leda and the Swan«, »Meru«), wogegen Eliot und Pound sich damit begnügten, in diesem Genre ihre Fingerübungen zu absolvieren.

Die besten englischen Sonettisten seit Yeats sind Campbell und Auden. Campbell hat, von zahlreichen eigenen Gedichten in diesem Genre abgesehen, über 100 Sonette aus den romanischen Sprachen übersetzt. Er bedient sich vorzugsweise des italienischen, Auden des englischen Typus. Was die Vielfalt ihrer Themen (Religion, Natur, Liebe, Kunst, Krieg, Politik) und die Virtuosität ihrer Versbehandlung betrifft, brauchen beide Dichter den Vergleich mit den größten ihrer Vorgänger nicht zu scheuen. Die übrigen hier vorgestellten Sonette des 20. Jahrhunderts belegen stellvertretend für viele andere, welche Faszination die Form – »that most taxing of sprints in the athletics of poetry« (Causley) – heute noch ausstrahlt.

Michael Hanke

Zitierte Literatur

Boswell, James, *The Life of Samuel Johnson* [gekürzt], hrsg. von Christopher Hibbert, Harmondsworth 1986 ([1]1979).

Bullock, Walter L., »The Genesis of the English Sonnet Form«, in: *Publications of the Modern Language Association* 38 (1923) S. 729–744.

Friedrich, Hugo, *Epochen der italienischen Lyrik*, Frankfurt a. M. 1964.

Fuller, John, *The Sonnet*, London 1972.

Peterson, Douglas L., *The English Lyric from Wyatt to Donne: A History of the Plain and Eloquent Styles*, Princeton [2]1991 ([1]1967).

Reichenberger, Kurt, »Francesco Petrarca«, in: *Die Großen der Weltgeschichte*, Bd. 3: *Harun ar-Raschid bis Petrarca*, Zürich 1973, S. 882–898.
Standop, Ewald, *Abriss der englischen Metrik*, Tübingen 1989.
Viebrock, Helmut, *John Keats*, Darmstadt 1977.

Who so list to hunt, I know where is an hind,
But as for me, alas, I may no more:
The vain travail hath wearied me so sore
I am of them that farthest cometh behind.
Yet may I by no means my wearied mind
Draw from the deer, but as she fleeth afore
Fainting I follow. I leave off therefore,
Since in a net I seek to hold the wind.
Who list her hunt, I put him out of doubt,
As well as I may spend his time in vain,
And graven with diamonds in letters plain
There is written, her fair neck round about:
"*Noli me tangere,* for Caesar's I am,
And wild for to hold, though I seem tame."

Freie Nachdichtung von Petrarcas *Rime* 190 (»Una candida cerva sopra l'erba«). 1 **who:** *he who.* **to list:** wünschen; belieben, gefallen. **hind:** Hirschkuh. 2 **alas:** ach! 3 **travail:** Mühe, Strapaze. 4 **cometh:** *come.* 6 **afore:** vor. 8 Sprichwörtliche Formulierung. 11 **graven:** eingraviert. 13 **Noli me tangere** (Lat.): Berühre mich nicht (vgl. Joh. 20,17).

The soote season, that bud and bloom forth brings,
With green hath clad the hill and eke the vale;
The nightingale with feathers new she sings,
The turtle to her make hath told her tale.
Summer is come, for every spray now springs;
The hart hath hung his old head on the pale,
The buck in brake his winter coat he flings,
The fishes float with new repairèd scale,
The adder all her slough away she slings,
The swift swallow pursueth the fliès small,
The busy bee her honey now she mings;
Winter is worn, that was the flowers' bale.
  And thus I see among these pleasant things,
  Each care decays, and yet my sorrow springs.

Freie Nachdichtung von Petrarcas *Rime* 310 (»Zefiro torna, e 'l bel tempo rimena«). 1 **soote:** süß, duftend. **to bring forth:** hervorbringen. 2 **clad:** Part. Perf. von *to clothe*. **eke:** auch. **vale:** Tal. 4 **turtle:** Turteltaube. **make:** *mate.* 5 **spray:** Zweig. 6 **hart:** Hirsch. **pale:** Pfahl. 7 **brake:** Dickicht. 8 **scale:** Schuppe. 9 **adder:** Natter. **slough:** abgestreifte Haut. 11 **to ming:** *to mingle.* 12 **bale:** Verderben.

The glorious image of the Maker's beauty,
My sovereign saint, the idol of my thought,
Dare not henceforth above the bounds of duty
T'accuse of pride, or rashly blame for aught.
For being, as she is, divinely wrought,
And of the brood of angels heavenly born,
And with the crew of blessèd saints upbrought,
Each of which did her with their gifts adorn;
The bud of joy, the blossom of the morn,
The beam of light, whom mortal eyes admire:
What reason is it then but she should scorn
Base things that to her love too bold aspire?
  Such heavenly forms ought rather worshipped be
  Than dare be loved by men of mean degree.

(*Amoretti* LXI) (c. 1594)

1 **Maker:** Schöpfer, Gott. 2 **idol:** verehrungswürdiges Bild einer Gottheit. 3 **dare:** *dare you.* **above the bounds of duty:** über das (von der höfischen Liebe) Geforderte hinaus. 4 **aught:** etwas. 5 **divinely** (adv.): göttlich. **wrought:** gemacht. 6 **brood:** Familie. 7 **to bring s.o. up:** jdn. er-, aufziehen. 8 **to adorn:** schmücken, zieren. 11 **but:** *that.* 12 **to aspire:** sich erheben. 13 **form:** körperliche Gestalt.

Loving in truth, and fain in verse my love to show,
That the dear She might take some pleasure of my pain:
Pleasure might cause her read, reading might make her know,
Knowledge might pity win, and pity grace obtain,
I sought fit words to paint the blackest face of woe,
Studying inventions fine, her wits to entertain:
Oft turning others' leaves, to see if thence would flow
Some fresh and fruitful showers upon my sun-burned brain.
But words came halting forth, wanting Invention's stay;
Invention, Nature's child, fled step-dame Study's blows,
And others' feet still seemed but strangers in my way.
Thus great with child to speak, and helpless in my throes,
Biting my truant pen, beating myself for spite,
"Fool," said my Muse to me, "look in thy heart and write."

(*Astrophel and Stella* I) (c. 1582)

1 **fain:** bereit. 4 **grace:** Erhörung. 5 **woe:** Leid, Elend. 6 **invention:** Sammeln rhetorischer Argumente. 9 **halting:** hinkend, lahmend. **wanting Invention's stay:** angewiesen auf die Stütze der *inventio.* 10 **step-dame:** Stiefmutter. 12 **great with child:** schwanger. **throes:** Geburtswehen. 13 **truant:** streikend, bummelnd. **spite:** Bosheit, Ärger.

With how sad steps, o Moon, thou climb'st the skies,
How silently, and with how wan a face!
What, may it be that even in heav'nly place
That busy archer his sharp arrows tries?
Sure, if that long-with-love-acquainted eyes
Can judge of Love, thou feel'st a Lover's case;
I read it in thy looks: thy languished grace
To me, that feel the like, thy state descries.
Then, ev'n of fellowship, o Moon, tell me,
Is constant love deemed there but want of wit?
Are beauties there as proud as here they be?
Do they above love to be loved, and yet
Those lovers scorn whom that love doth possess?
Do they call virtue there ungratefulness?

(*Astrophel and Stella* XXXI) (c. 1582)

2 **wan:** bleich. 4 **archer:** Bogenschütze (Cupido). 5 **if that:** *if.* 7 **languished:** krank, schmachtend. 8 **to descry:** erkennen lassen. 9 **ev'n of fellowship:** vom gleichen Schicksal getroffen. 10 **to deem:** (für etwas) halten. **want of wit:** Einfallslosigkeit. 14 **Do they call … ungratefulness?:** *Do they call ungratefulness a virtue there?*

When men shall find thy flower, thy glory pass,
And thou, with careful brow sitting alone,
Receivèd hast this message from thy glass,
That tells thee truth, and says that all is gone,
Fresh shalt thou see in me the wounds thou madest,
Though spent thy flame, in me the heat remaining,
I that have loved thee thus before thou fadest,
My faith shall wax, when thou art in thy waning.
The world shall find this miracle in me,
That fire can burn when all the matter's spent;
Then what my faith hath been thyself shalt see,
And that thou wast unkind thou mayst repent.
  Thou mayst repent, that thou hast scorned my tears,
  When winter snows upon thy golden hairs.

(*Delia* XXXIII) (publ. 1592)

2 **careful:** besorgt, sorgenvoll. **brow:** Stirn, Gesicht. 8 **to wax:** wachsen, zunehmen. **to wane:** abnehmen (Mond). 12 **to repent:** bereuen.

Since there's no help, come let us kiss and part;
Nay, I have done: you get no more of me,
And I am glad, yea, glad with all my heart
That thus so cleanly I myself can free;
Shake hands for ever, cancel all our vows,
And when we meet at any time again,
Be it not seen in either of our brows
That we one jot of former love retain.
Now at the last gasp of Love's latest breath,
When, his pulse failing, Passion speechless lies,
When Faith is kneeling by his bed of death,
And Innocence is closing up his eyes,
  Now if thou wouldst, when all have given him over,
  From death to life thou mightst him yet recover.

(*Idea* LXI) (publ. 1619)

4 **cleanly** (adv.): voll und ganz. 7 **brow:** Gesicht. 8 **one jot:** das kleinste bisschen. 13 **to give s.o. over:** jdn. aufgeben.

Shall I compare thee to a summer's day?
Thou art more lovely and more temperate.
Rough winds do shake the darling buds of May,
And summer's lease hath all too short a date.
Sometime too hot the eye of heaven shines,
And often is his gold complexion dimmed;
And every fair from fair sometime declines,
By chance or nature's changing course untrimmed.
But thy eternal summer shall not fade,
Nor lose possession of that fair thou ow'st,
Nor shall Death brag thou wand'rest in his shade,
When in eternal lines to time thou grow'st.
So long as men can breathe or eyes can see,
So long lives this, and this gives life to thee.

(*Sonnets* XVIII)

2 **temperate:** ausgeglichen. 4 **lease:** Pachtzeit. **date:** Dauer. 6 **complexion:** Teint. 7 **fair:** Schönheit. 8 **untrimmed:** der Schönheit beraubt. 10 **to owe:** besitzen. 11 **to brag:** prahlen. 12 **lines** (pl.): Dichtung; Abstammung. 14 **this:** Gemeint ist das Gedicht.

When, in disgrace with Fortune and men's eyes,
I all alone beweep my outcast state,
And trouble deaf heaven with my bootless cries,
And look upon myself and curse my fate,
Wishing me like to one more rich in hope,
Featured like him, like him with friends possessed,
Desiring this man's art, and that man's scope,
With what I most enjoy contented least;
Yet, in these thoughts myself almost despising,
Haply I think on thee, and then my state,
Like to the lark at break of day arising
From sullen earth, sings hymns at heaven's gate;
  For thy sweet love remembered such wealth brings
  That then I scorn to change my state with kings.

(*Sonnets* XXIX)

1 **disgrace:** Ungnade, Unehre. 2 **outcast:** verstoßen. 3 **bootless:** vergeblich. 6 **featured:** gestaltet. 7 **scope:** Wirkungskreis, Spielraum. 10 **haply** (adv.): zufällig, vielleicht. 12 **sullen:** düster. 14 **with kings:** *with that of kings.*

Since brass, nor stone, nor earth, nor boundless sea,
But sad mortality o'ersways their power,
How with this rage shall beauty hold a plea,
Whose action is no stronger than a flower?
O, how shall summer's honey breath hold out
Against the wrackful siege of battering days,
When rocks impregnable are not so stout,
Nor gates of steel so strong, but Time decays?
O, fearful meditation! Where, alack,
Shall Time's best jewel from Time's chest lie hid?
Or what strong hand can hold his swift foot back?
Or who his spoil of beauty can forbid?
  O, none, unless this miracle have might,
  That in black ink my love may still shine bright.

(*Sonnets* LXV)

1 f.: »Since *there is* neither brass nor stone, neither earth nor boundless sea except [of a kind that] their power is overcome by mortality« (Standop). 2 **sad:** traurig machend. 3 **with:** gegen. **to hold a plea:** plädieren. 6 **wrackful:** zugrunde richtend. **to batter:** zerschmettern. 7 **impregnable:** uneinnehmbar. 8 **decays:** *decays them.* 9 **fearful:** ängstlich. **alack:** o weh! 10 **chest:** (Schatz-)Truhe; (Juwelen-)Schatulle. 12 **to forbid:** abwenden, verhindern.

That time of year thou mayst in me behold
When yellow leaves, or none, or few, do hang
Upon those boughs which shake against the cold,
Bare ruined choirs where late the sweet birds sang.
In me thou seest the twilight of such day
As after sunset fadeth in the west,
Which by and by black night doth take away,
Death's second self, that seals up all in rest.
In me thou seest the glowing of such fire
That on the ashes of his youth doth lie,
As the deathbed whereon it must expire,
Consumed with that which it was nourished by.
  This thou perceiv'st, which makes thy love more strong,
  To love that well which thou must leave ere long.

(*Sonnets* LXXIII)

4 **choir:** Chorraum (einer Kirche). **late:** vor kurzem. 5 **the twilight of such day:** *such a twilight of the day.* 7 **by and by:** bald. 8 **to seal up:** versiegeln. 10 **his:** *its.* 11 **to expire:** sterben. 12 **to consume:** verzehren. **to nourish:** nähren. 14 **ere long:** demnächst, bald.

Let me not to the marriage of true minds
Admit impediments; love is not love
Which alters when it alteration finds,
Or bends with the remover to remove.
O no, it is an ever-fixèd mark
That looks on tempests and is never shaken;
It is the star to every wandering bark,
Whose worth's unknown, although his height be taken.
Love's not Time's fool, though rosy lips and cheeks
Within his bending sickle's compass come;
Love alters not with his brief hours and weeks,
But bears it out even to the edge of doom.
  If this be error and upon me proved,
  I never writ, nor no man ever loved.

(*Sonnets* CXVI)

2 **impediment:** Hindernis (vgl. die Formel der Hochzeitsliturgie: »If any of you know cause or just impediment why these persons should not be joined together«). 4 **to remove:** sich entfernen. 5 **mark:** Seezeichen. 7 **star:** Polarstern. **bark:** Barke, Boot. 10 **sickle:** Sichel. **compass:** Umkreis. 12 **to bear s.th. out:** etwas aushalten, ertragen. **doom:** Untergang; Jüngstes Gericht. 13 **to prove s.th. upon s.o.:** jdm. etwas beweisen. 14 **writ:** *wrote.* **nor no man:** und niemand.

Th'expense of spirit in a waste of shame
Is lust in action, and, till action, lust
Is perjured, murd'rous, bloody, full of blame,
Savage, extreme, rude, cruel, not to trust,
Enjoyed no sooner but despisèd straight,
Past reason hunted, and no sooner had,
Past reason hated as a swallowed bait
On purpose laid to make the taker mad;
Mad in pursuit, and in possession so,
Had, having, and in quest to have, extreme,
A bliss in proof, and proved, a very woe,
Before, a joy proposed, behind, a dream.
  All this the world well knows, yet none knows well
  To shun the heaven that leads men to this hell.

(*Sonnets* CXXIX)

1 **expense:** Ausgabe, Verschwendung. **a waste of shame:** *a shameful waste.* 3 **perjured:** ehrlos, verlogen. 4 **extreme:** maßlos. **not to trust:** verräterisch. 7 **to swallow:** verschlucken. **bait:** Köder. 10 **in quest:** auf der Suche. 11 **bliss:** Wonne, Entzücken. **in proof:** im Vollzug. **woe:** Leid, Elend. 12 **to propose:** in Aussicht stellen. 14 **to shun s.th.:** sich von etwas fernhalten.

My mistress' eyes are nothing like the sun;
Coral is far more red than her lips' red;
If snow be white, why then her breasts are dun;
If hairs be wires, black wires grow on her head.
I have seen roses damasked, red and white,
But no such roses see I in her cheeks,
And in some perfumes is there more delight
Than in the breath that from my mistress reeks.
I love to hear her speak, yet well I know
That music hath a far more pleasing sound.
I grant I never saw a goddess go;
My mistress when she walks treads on the ground.
  And yet, by heaven, I think my love as rare
  As any she belied with false compare.

(*Sonnets* CXXX)

1 **nothing like:** in keiner Weise vergleichbar. 3 **dun:** graubraun. 4 **black wires:** Verballhornung des Klischeevergleichs von Frauenhaar mit goldenem Draht. 5 **damasked:** damaszenerrot. 8 **to reek:** aushauchen, -strömen. 11 **I never saw a goddess go:** Die Füße der Göttin Ate berührten den Boden nicht (vgl. *Ilias* XIX,92). 13 **rare:** prächtig. 14 **any she belied:** jede Frau, über die man Lügen verbreitet.

Poor soul, the centre of my sinful earth,
[Fooled by] these rebel powers that thee array,
Why dost thou pine within and suffer dearth,
Painting thy outward walls so costly gay?
Why so large cost, having so short a lease,
Dost thou upon thy fading mansion spend?
Shall worms, inheritors of this excess,
Eat up thy charge? Is this thy body's end?
Then, soul, live thou upon thy servant's loss,
And let that pine to aggravate thy store;
Buy terms divine in selling hours of dross;
Within be fed, without be rich no more:
So shalt thou feed on Death, that feeds on men,
And Death once dead there's no more dying then.

(*Sonnets* CXLVI) (publ. 1609)

2 **[Fooled by]:** Die Quarto-Version weist eine Wiederholung der Schlussworte von Z. 1 (»My sinful earth«) auf; die Emendation »Fooled by« wurde erstmals 1780 von Malone vorgeschlagen. Weitere Emendationsversuche: »Tricked by« (Latham Davis), »Starved by [the]« (Steevens), »Gulled by« (Seymour-Smith). **to array:** kleiden. 3 **dearth:** Not, Mangel. 5 **lease:** Pachtzeit. 6 **mansion:** (herrschaftliches) Haus. 7 **excess:** Verschwendung. 8 **charge:** Aufwendungen. 9 **upon thy servant's loss:** auf Kosten deines Dieners (d. h. des Körpers). 10 **that:** bezogen auf *servant.* **to aggravate:** vergrößern. **store:** Reichtum, Vorrat. 11 **buy terms divine:** erwirb dir die himmlische Ewigkeit. **dross:** wertloses Gut.

At the round earth's imagined corners, blow
Your trumpets, angels, and arise, arise
From death, you numberless infinities
Of souls, and to your scattered bodies go,
All whom the flood did, and fire shall o'erthrow,
All whom war, dearth, age, agues, tyrannies,
Despair, law, chance, hath slain, and you whose eyes,
Shall behold God, and never taste death's woe.
But let them sleep, Lord, and me mourn a space,
For, if above all these, my sins abound,
'Tis late to ask abundance of thy grace,
When we are there; here on this lowly ground,
Teach me how to repent; for that's as good
As if thou hadst sealed my pardon, with thy blood.

(*Holy Sonnets* VII) (c. 1609)

1 Vgl. Offb. 7,1 (»And after these things I saw four angels standing on the four corners of the earth, holding the four winds of the earth«). 5 **flood:** Sintflut. **fire:** Gemeint ist das Feuer der Endzeit. 6 **dearth:** Hungersnot. **agues** (pl.): Schüttelfrost. 7 f. Vgl. 1 Kor. 15,51 f. (»We shall not all sleep, but we shall all be changed, in a moment, in the twinkling of an eye, at the last trump«). 8 **woe:** Leid, Elend. 9 **to mourn:** trauern. **a space:** eine Weile. 10 **to abound:** reichlich vorhanden sein. 12 **lowly:** niedrig. 13 **to repent:** bereuen. 14 **to seal:** besiegeln; bekräftigen.

Death be not proud, thou some have callèd thee
Mighty and dreadful, for, thou art not so,
For, those, whom thou think'st, thou dost overthrow,
Die not, poor death, nor yet canst thou kill me;
From rest and sleep, which but thy pictures be,
Much pleasure, then from thee, much more must flow,
And soonest our best men with thee do go,
Rest of their bones, and soul's delivery.
Thou art slave to fate, chance, kings, and desperate men,
And dost with poison, war, and sickness dwell,
And poppy, or charms can make us sleep as well,
And better than thy stroke; why swell'st thou then?
One short sleep past, we wake eternally,
And death shall be no more, Death thou shalt die.

(*Holy Sonnets* X) (c. 1609)

6 **much pleasure:** *much pleasure flows.* 10 **to dwell:** verweilen. 11 **poppy:** Mohn. 12 **to swell:** großtun, sich aufblasen. 14 Vgl. 1 Kor. 15,26 und 15,54 (»The last enemy that shall be destroyed is death [...] Death is swallowed up in victory«).

Batter my heart, three-personed God; for, you
As yet but knock, breathe, shine, and seek to mend;
That I may rise, and stand, o'erthrow me, and bend
Your force, to break, blow, burn, and make me new.
I, like an usurped town, to another due,
Labour to admit you, but oh, to no end,
Reason your viceroy in me, me should defend,
But is captived, and proves weak or untrue,
Yet dearly I love you, and would be loved fain,
But am betrothed unto your enemy,
Divorce me, untie, or break that knot again,
Take me to you, imprison me, for I
Except you enthral me, never shall be free,
Nor ever chaste, except you ravish me.

(*Holy Sonnets* XIV) (c. 1609)

1 **to batter:** zerschmettern. 2 **to mend:** flicken. 3 **to bend:** neigen. 4 **to blow:** niederschlagen, umblasen. 5 **to usurp:** besetzen. **to another due:** einem anderen gehörend. 6 **to labour:** sich mühen. **to admit:** einlassen. **to no end:** vergebens. 7 **viceroy:** Vizekönig. 8 **captived:** gefangen gesetzt. 9 **fain:** gern. 10 **betrothed:** verlobt. 13 **to enthral:** versklaven. 14 **chaste:** keusch. **to ravish:** vergewaltigen.

Redemption

Having been tenant long to a rich Lord,
  Not thriving, I resolvèd to be bold,
  And make a suit unto him, to afford
A new small-rented lease, and cancel th' old.
In heaven at his manor I him sought:
  They told me there, that he was lately gone
  About some land, which he had dearly bought
Long since on earth, to take possession.
I straight return'd, and knowing his great birth,
  Sought him accordingly in great resorts;
  In cities, theatres, gardens, parks, and courts:
At length I heard a ragged noise and mirth
  Of theeves and murderers: there I him espied,
  Who straight, "Your suit is granted," said, & died.

[Titel] **redemption: 1.** Rückkauf, Freikauf von Schuld; **2.** Erlösung. 1 **tenant:** Pächter. **Lord:** Grundherr. 2 **to thrive:** reich werden, vorankommen. 3 **to make a suit:** Gesuch, Klage einreichen. 4 **small-rented lease:** billige Pacht. **to cancel:** annullieren. 5 **manor:** Herrenhaus. 7 **dearly** (adv.): teuer. 9 **straight:** unverzüglich. 10 **resort:** Erholungsort. 12 **ragged:** misstönend. **mirth:** Fröhlichkeit. 13 **to espy:** erspähen. 14 **Your suit is granted:** Anspielung auf Christus und den reumütigen Verbrecher am Kreuz (vgl. Lk. 23,39 ff.).

When I consider how my light is spent,
Ere half my days, in this dark world and wide,
And that one talent which is death to hide,
Lodged with me useless, though my soul more bent
To serve therewith my maker, and present
My true account, lest he returning chide,
"Doth God exact day-labour, light denied?"
I fondly ask; but Patience to prevent
That murmur, soon replies, "God doth not need
Either man's work or his own gifts, who best
Bear his mild yoke, they serve him best, his state
Is kingly. Thousands at his bidding speed
And post o'er land and ocean without rest:
They also serve who only stand and wait."

1 **light:** Sehkraft. Milton erblindete 1652. 2 **ere half my days:** vor Ablauf meiner halben Lebenszeit (vgl. Plato, *Rep.* 615, Ps. 90,10). 3 **that one talent:** Vgl. Mt. 25,14 ff. und Luk. 19,12 ff. 4 **to lodge:** wohnen. **bent:** bestrebt. 5 **maker:** Gott, Schöpfer. 6 **to chide:** schelten. 7 **to exact:** fordern. **day-labour**: Vgl. Joh. 9,4. **light denied:** *if light is denied.* 8 **fondly** (adv.): töricht. **to prevent**: vorwegnehmen, vereiteln. 9 **murmur:** Murren. 10 **gifts:** Gaben, Talente, die Gott dem Menschen verliehen hat. 11 **his mild yoke:** Vgl. Mt. 11,30 (»For my yoke is easy, and my burden is light«). 12 **thousands:** Gemeint sind die Engel (vgl. Ps. 68,17). **bidding:** Befehl. 13 **to post:** eilen. 14 Vgl. Lk. 1,19 (»And the angel answering said unto him, I am Gabriel that stand in the presence of God«).

On the late Massacre in Piedmont

Avenge O Lord thy slaughtered saints, whose bones
  Lie scattered on the Alpine mountains cold,
  Even them who kept thy truth so pure of old
  When all our fathers worshipped stocks and stones,
Forget not: in thy book record their groans
  Who were thy sheep and in their ancient fold
  Slain by the bloody Piedmontese that rolled
  Mother with infant down the rocks. Their moans
The vales redoubled to the hills, and they
  To heaven. Their martyred blood and ashes sow
  O'er all the Italian fields where still doth sway
The triple Tyrant: that from these may grow
  A hundredfold, who having learnt thy way
  Early may fly the Babylonian woe.

(c. 1655)

[Titel] Am 24. April 1655 ließ der Herzog von Savoyen im Piemont 300 Waldenser ermorden, weil sie sich weigerten zu konvertieren. 1 **to avenge:** rächen (vgl. Ps. 78,2 und 78,10 sowie Offb. 6,9 f.) 4 **to worship:** anbeten. **stocks and stones:** Heiligenbilder aus Holz und Stein. 5 **book:** Buch des Lebens (vgl. Offb. 5,1 ff.). 6 **fold:** Schafhürde; (kirchliche) Gemeinde. 9 **vale:** Tal. **to redouble:** doppelt widerhallen. 10 Vgl. Tertullian, *Apologeticus* 50. 11 **to sway:** herrschen. 12 **the triple Tyrant:** Gemeint ist der Papst. 13 **a hundredfold:** hundertmal so viele. 14 **the Babylonian woe:** Vgl. Offb. 17; von puritanischen Autoren wird die Stelle gern auf die katholische Kirche bezogen (*woe:* Leid, Elend).

Methought I saw my late espousèd saint
  Brought to me like Alcestis from the grave,
  Whom Jove's great son to her glad husband gave,
  Rescued from death by force though pale and faint.
Mine as whom washed from spot of childbed taint,
  Purification in the old Law did save,
  And such, as yet once more I trust to have
  Full sight of her in heaven without restraint,
Came vested all in white, pure as her mind:
  Her face was veiled, yet to my fancied sight,
  Love, sweetness, goodness in her person shined
So clear, as in no face with more delight.
  But O as to embrace me she inclined
  I waked, she fled, and day brought back my night.

1 **my late espoused saint:** Gemeint ist entweder Miltons erste Frau Mary Powell, die 1652 während der Geburt eines Kindes starb, oder seine zweite Frau, Katherine Woodcock, die im Februar 1658, einige Monate nach der Geburt ihres ersten Kindes, starb; zur Vision der toten Geliebten vgl. Properz, Elegie 4,7 (*espoused:* verheiratet). 2 **Alcestis:** Figur der griechischen Mythologie, die für ihren Mann Admet starb und von Herkules aus der Unterwelt befreit wurde. 3 **Jove's great son:** Herkules (*Jove:* Jupiter). 5 **as whom:** *as one whom.* 6 Vgl. 3. Mose 12. **purification:** Reinigung, Läuterung. 10 **veiled:** Auch Alkestis kehrte verschleiert zurück. **to my fancied sight:** meinem Vorstellungsvermögen. 13 **to incline:** sich neigen.

Sonnet on the Death of Mr Richard West

In vain to me the smiling mornings shine,
And reddening Phoebus lifts his golden fire:
The birds in vain their amorous descant join,
Or cheerful fields resume their green attire:
These ears, alas! for other notes repine,
A different object do these eyes require.
My lonely anguish melts no heart but mine;
And in my breast the imperfect joys expire.
Yet morning smiles the busy race to cheer,
And new-born pleasure brings to happier men:
The fields to all their wonted tribute bear;
To warm their little loves the birds complain.
I fruitless mourn to him that cannot hear,
And weep the more because I weep in vain.

(c. 1742)

[Titel] Grays Freund Richard West starb 1742. 2 **Phoebus:** Sonnengott (Apollo). 3 **amorous descant:** verliebter Gesang (vgl. Miltons *Paradise Lost* IV,603). 4 **to resume:** wieder aufnehmen. **attire:** Kleidung. 5 **alas:** ach! **to repine:** klagen. 7 **anguish:** Schmerz. 8 **to expire:** sterben. 9 **the busy race:** Gemeint ist die Menschheit. 11 **wonted:** gewohnt; üblich. 12 **to warm:** erwärmen, anregen. **to complain:** klagen, singen. 13 **to mourn:** trauern.

Composed upon Westminster Bridge, September 3, 1802

Earth has not anything to show more fair:
Dull would he be of soul who could pass by
A sight so touching in its majesty:
This City now doth, like a garment, wear
The beauty of the morning; silent, bare,
Ships, towers, domes, theatres, and temples lie
Open unto the fields, and to the sky;
All bright and glittering in the smokeless air.
Never did sun more beautifully steep
In his first splendour, valley, rock, or hill;
Ne'er saw I, never felt, a calm so deep!
The river glideth at his own sweet will:
Dear God! the very houses seem asleep;
And all that mighty heart is lying still!

[Titel] Anmerkung des Dichters: »Composed on the roof of a coach, on my way to France Sept. 1802.« Möglicherweise ist das Sonett schon am 31. Juli 1802 entstanden. 4 **garment:** Gewand. 6 **dome:** Kuppel. 9 **to steep:** eintauchen. 10 **splendour:** Glanz.

London, 1802

Milton! thou shouldst be living at this hour:
England hath need of thee: she is a fen
Of stagnant waters: altar, sword, and pen,
Fireside, the heroic wealth of hall and bower,
Have forfeited their ancient English dower
Of inward happiness. We are selfish men;
Oh! raise us up, return to us again;
And give us manners, virtue, freedom, power.
Thy soul was like a Star, and dwelt apart;
Thou hadst a voice whose sound was like the sea:
Pure as the naked heavens, majestic, free,
So didst thou travel on life's common way,
In cheerful godliness; and yet thy heart
The lowliest duties on herself did lay.

(c. 1802)

2 **fen:** Sumpf. 3 **stagnant:** stehend, abgestanden. 4 **fireside:** Kamin; Familienkreis. **bower:** Laube. 5 **to forfeit:** verwirken, verlieren. **dower:** Mitgift. 8 **manners:** Sitten. 9 **to dwell:** verweilen. 13 **godliness:** Frömmigkeit, Gottesfurcht. 14 **lowly:** niedrig.

Surprised by joy – impatient as the Wind
I turned to share the transport – Oh! with whom
But Thee, deep buried in the silent tomb,
That spot which no vicissitude can find?
Love, faithful love, recalled thee to my mind –
But how could I forget thee? Through what power,
Even for the least division of an hour,
Have I been so beguiled as to be blind
To my most grievous loss! – That thought's return
Was the worst pang that sorrow ever bore,
Save one, one only, when I stood forlorn,
Knowing my heart's best treasure was no more;
That neither present time, nor years unborn
Could to my sight that heavenly face restore.

(c. 1812?, publ. 1815)

2 **transport:** Entzücken. 3 **tomb:** Grab. 4 **vicissitude:** Schicksalsschlag. 8 **to beguile:** bezaubern. 9 **grievous:** schmerzlich, bedrückend. 10 **pang:** Pein. 14 **to restore:** zurückbringen, wiedergeben.

Ozymandias

I met a traveller from an antique land
Who said: Two vast and trunkless legs of stone
Stand in the desert . . . Near them, on the sand,
Half sunk, a shattered visage lies, whose frown,
And wrinkled lip, and sneer of cold command,
Tell that its sculptor well those passions read
Which yet survive, stamped on these lifeless things,
The hand that mocked them, and the heart that fed:
And on the pedestal these words appear:
"My name is Ozymandias, king of kings:
Look on my works, ye Mighty, and despair!"
Nothing beside remains. Round the decay
Of that colossal wreck, boundless and bare
The lone and level sands stretch far away.

(c. 1817)

[Titel] **Ozymandias:** Ramses II. 2 **trunkless legs** (pl.): ohne Oberkörper (vgl. Dan. 2,33 f.). 4 **to shatter:** zerbrechen, zerschmettern. 5 **wrinkled:** geschrumpft. **sneer:** Hohnlächeln, verächtliche Äußerung. 8 **to mock: 1.** nachahmen; **2.** verhöhnen. 9 **pedestal:** Sockel. 10 f. Richard Pococke (*A Description of the East*, 1743) gibt die Inschrift der Ozymandias-Statue so wieder: »I am the king of kings, Osymanduas: If anyone would know how great I am, and where I lie, let him exceed the works that I have done.« 13 **boundless:** grenzenlos. 14 **lone:** *lonely.*

The Thrush's Nest

Within a thick and spreading hawthorn bush
That overhung a mole-hill large and round,
I heard from morn to morn a merry thrush
Sing hymns to sunrise, while I drank the sound
With joy; and, often an intruding guest,
I watched her secret toils from day to day –
How true she warped the moss to form a nest,
And modelled it within with wood and clay;
And by and by, like heath-bells gilt with dew,
There lay her shining eggs, as bright as flowers,
Ink-spotted over shells of greeny blue;
And there I witnessed, in the sunny hours,
A brood of nature's minstrels chirp and fly,
Glad as that sunshine and the laughing sky.

(publ. 1835)

1 **hawthorn:** Hagedorn. 2 **mole-hill:** Maulwurfshügel. 5 **to intrude:** sich auf-, eindrängen, stören. 6 **toil:** Mühe. 7 **to warp:** formen. 9 **heath-bells** (pl.): Sumpfheide. **gilt:** vergoldet, glänzend. 13 **brood:** Brut. **minstrel:** (Minne-)Sänger, Spielmann. **to chirp:** zwitschern.

On First Looking into Chapman's Homer

Much have I travelled in the realms of gold,
And many goodly states and kingdoms seen;
Round many western islands have I been
Which bards in fealty to Apollo hold.
Oft of one wide expanse had I been told
That deep-browed Homer ruled as his demesne;
Yet did I never breathe its pure serene
Till I heard Chapman speak out loud and bold:
Then felt I like some watcher of the skies
When a new planet swims into his ken;
Or like stout Cortez when with eagle eyes
He stared at the Pacific – and all his men
Looked at each other with a wild surmise –
Silent, upon a peak in Darien.

(c. 1816)

[Titel] **Chapman:** George Ch. (um 1559–1634), englischer Lyriker und Dramatiker; Verfasser der ersten vollständigen englischen Homer-Übersetzung. 1 **realm:** Reich. 2 **goodly:** ansehnlich, herrlich. 4 **bard:** Barde, Sänger; Dichter. **in fealty:** in Lehenstreue. 5 **oft:** *often.* **expanse:** weite Fläche. 6 **demesne:** Domäne. 7 **pure serene:** klarer Himmel. 10 **a new planet:** 1781 hatte F. W. Herschel den Planeten Uranus entdeckt. **ken:** Gesichtskreis. 11 **Cortez:** Nicht Cortez, sondern Bilbao entdeckte 1513 den Pazifik. 13 **surmise:** Vermutung. 14 **Darien:** Darién, Landschaft in Zentralamerika.

On Seeing the Elgin Marbles

My spirit is too weak – mortality
Weighs heavily on me like unwilling sleep,
And each imagined pinnacle and steep
Of godlike hardship, tells me I must die
Like a sick Eagle looking at the sky.
Yet 'tis a gentle luxury to weep
That I have not the cloudy winds to keep
Fresh for the opening of the morning's eye.
Such dim-conceivèd glories of the brain
Bring round the heart an undescribable feud;
So do these wonders a most dizzy pain,
That mingles Grecian grandeur with the rude
Wasting of old Time – with a billowy main –
A sun – a shadow of a magnitude.

(c. 1817)

[Titel] **Elgin Marbles:** phidianische Skulpturen und Reliefs, die vom Kunstliebhaber Lord Elgin nach England gebracht wurden; Keats sah sie 1817 im Britischen Museum. 1 **mortality:** Sterblichkeit. 2 **to weigh on s.o.:** auf jdm. lasten, jdn. belasten. 3 **pinnacle:** Zinne; Gipfel. **steep:** Steilhang. 4 **hardship:** Bedrängnis, Mühsal. 6 **luxury:** Freude. 9 **dim-conceived:** vage wahrgenommen. 10 **feud:** Fehde. 11 **dizzy:** Schwindel erregend. 13 **wasting:** Verlust, Schwinden. **billowy:** schwellend, wogend. **main:** Meer.

Bright star! would I were steadfast as thou art –
Not in lone splendour hung aloft the night
And watching, with eternal lids apart,
Like nature's patient, sleepless Eremite,
The moving waters at their priestlike task
Of pure ablution round earth's human shores,
Or gazing on the new soft-fallen mask
Of snow upon the mountains and the moors –
No – yet still steadfast, still unchangeable,
Pillowed upon my fair love's ripening breast,
To feel for ever its soft swell and fall,
Awake for ever in a sweet unrest,
Still, still to hear her tender-taken breath,
And so live ever – or else swoon to death.

(c. 1818 or 1819)

1 **steadfast:** beständig. 2 **lone:** *lonely.* **aloft:** hoch oben in. 4 **eremite:** *hermit:* Einsiedler. 6 **ablution:** (rituelle) Waschung. 10 **pillowed:** gebettet. 13 **tender-taken:** sanft geschöpft. 14 **to swoon:** ohnmächtig werden.

If thou must love me, let it be for nought
Except for love's sake only. Do not say
"I love her for her smile – her look – her way
Of speaking gently, – for a trick of thought
That falls in well with mine, and certes brought
A sense of pleasant ease on such a day" –
For these things in themselves, Belovèd, may
Be changed, or change for thee, – and love, so wrought,
May be unwrought so. Neither love me for
Thine own dear pity's wiping my cheeks dry –
A creature might forget to weep, who bore
Thy comfort long, and lose thy love thereby!
But love me for love's sake, that evermore
Thou mayst love on, through love's eternity.

(*Sonnets from the Portuguese* XIV) (c. 1845/46)

1 **nought:** nichts. 4 **trick:** Kunstgriff, Eigenart. 5 **to fall in with s.th.:** mit etwas übereinstimmen. **certes:** sicherlich. 8 **wrought:** gemacht, gearbeitet. 12 **comfort:** Trost, Stärke. 13 **evermore:** für immer.

Dawn on the Night-journey

Till dawn the wind drove round me. It is past
   And still, and leaves the air to lisp of bird,
   And to the quiet that is almost heard
Of the new-risen day, as yet bound fast
In the first warmth of sunrise. When the last
   Of the sun's hours to-day shall be fulfilled,
   There shall another breath of time be stilled
For me, which now is to my senses cast
As much beyond me as eternity,
   Unknown, kept secret. On the newborn air
The moth quivers in silence. It is vast,
Yea, even beyond the hills upon the sea,
   The day whose end shall give this hour as sheer
As chaos to the irrevocable Past.

(c. 1855)

2 **to lisp:** lispeln. 11 **to quiver:** zucken, beben. 13 **sheer:** rein, gänzlich; unverfälscht. 14 **irrevocable:** unwiderruflich.

From Sunset to Star Rise

Go from me, summer friends, and tarry not:
  I am no summer friend, but wintry cold,
  A silly sheep benighted from the fold,
A sluggard with a thorn-choked garden plot.
Take counsel, sever from my lot your lot,
  Dwell in your pleasant places, hoard your gold;
  Lest you with me should shiver on the wold,
Athirst and hungering on a barren spot.
For I have hedged me with a thorny hedge,
  I live alone, I look to die alone:
Yet sometimes when a wind sighs through the sedge
  Ghosts of my buried years and friends come back,
My heart goes sighing after swallows flown
  On sometime summer's unreturning track.

(c. 1865)

1 **to tarry:** zögern, säumen. 3 **benighted:** von der Nacht überfallen. **fold:** Schafhürde; (kirchliche) Gemeinde. 4 **sluggard:** Faulpelz. **thorn-choked:** von Dornhecken überwuchert. 5 **counsel:** Ratschlag. **to sever:** (ab)trennen. **lot:** Los, Geschick. 6 **to dwell:** wohnen, sich aufhalten. **pleasant places:** Vgl. Ps. 16,6. **to hoard:** aufhäufen. 7 **wold:** Hügel-, Moor-, Heideland. 8 **athirst:** *thirsty.* **barren:** unfruchtbar, trocken. 11 **sedge:** Schilfgras. 14 **track:** Spur; Pfad.

"Or puoi la quantitate
Comprender de l'amor che a te mi scalda." – DANTE
"Non vo'che de tal nodo amor mi scioglia." – PETRARCA

Trust me, I have not earned your dear rebuke,
I love, as you would have me, God the most;
Would lose not Him, but you, must one be lost,
Nor with Lot's wife cast back a faithless look
Unready to forego what I forsook;
This say I, having counted up the cost,
This, though I be the feeblest of God's host,
The sorriest sheep Christ shepherds with His crook.
Yet while I love my God the most, I deem
That I can never love you overmuch;
I love Him more, so let me love you too;
Yea, as I apprehend it, love is such
I cannot love you if I love not Him,
I cannot love Him if I love not you.

(*Monna Innominata* VI) (1868?)

[Motti] »Heute kannst du die Menge der Liebe dir gegenüber, die mich erwärmt, verstehen« (Dante). – »Ich will nicht, daß die Liebe mich von solch einer Bindung befreit« (Petrarca). 4 **Lot:** biblische Gestalt (vgl. 1. Mose 19,15–26). 5 **to forego s.th.:** von etwas lassen. **to foresake:** aufgeben. 8 **sorry:** armselig. **crook:** Hirtenstab. 9 **to deem:** glauben. 12 **to apprehend:** begreifen, verstehen.

A Church Romance

(Mellstock: circa 1835)

She turned in the high pew, until her sight
Swept the west gallery, and caught its row
Of music-men with viol, book, and bow
Against the sinking sad tower-window light.

She turned again; and in her pride's despite
One strenuous viol's inspirer seemed to throw
A message from his string to her below,
Which said: "I claim thee as my own forthright!"

Thus their hearts' bond began, in due time signed.
And long years thence, when Age had scared Romance,
At some old attitude of his or glance
That gallery-scene would break upon her mind,
With him as minstrel, ardent, young, and trim,
Bowing "New Sabbath" or "Mount Ephraim."

(publ. 1906)

[Untertitel] **Mellstock:** Ort der ersten Begegnung von Hardys Eltern. 1 **pew:** Kirchenstuhl, -bank. 2 **gallery:** Empore. 3 **viol:** Viola, Gambe. 5 **in despite:** zum Trotz. 6 **strenuous:** emsig, energisch. **forthright:** freimütig. 10 **thence:** seit jener Zeit. **to break upon s.th.:** plötzlich über etwas hereinbrechen. 13 **minstrel:** (Minne-)Sänger, Spielmann. **ardent:** inbrünstig. **trim:** schmuck. 14 **"New Sabbath" / "Mount Ephraim":** Kirchenlieder.

Justus quidem tu es, Domine, si disputem tecum; verumtamen justa loquar ad te: Quare via impiorum prosperatur? Etc.

Thou art indeed just, Lord, if I contend
With thee; but, sir, so what I plead is just.
Why do sinners' ways prosper? and why must
Disappointment all I endeavour end?
  Wert thou my enemy, O thou my friend,
How wouldst thou worse, I wonder, than thou dost
Defeat, thwart me? Oh, the sots and thralls of lust
Do in spare hours more thrive than I that spend,
Sir, life upon thy cause. See, banks and brakes
Now, leavèd how thick! lacèd they are again
With fretty chervil, look, and fresh wind shakes
Them; birds build – but not I build; no, but strain,
Time's eunuch, and not breed one work that wakes.
Mine, O thou lord of life, send my roots rain.

(c. 1889)

[Motto] Vgl. Jer. 12,1 (»Righteous art thou, O Lord, when I plead with thee; yet let me talk with thee of thy judgements: Wherefore doth the way of the wicked prosper? Wherefore are all they happy that deal very treacherously?«). 1 **to contend:** rechten. 3 **to prosper:** gedeihen, Erfolg haben. 4 **to endeavour:** streben, (ver)suchen. 7 **to defeat:** besiegen. **to thwart:** behindern; vereiteln. **sot:** Säufer. **thrall:** Leibeigener; Sklave. 8 **to thrive:** gedeihen, vorwärtskommen. 9 **cause:** Sache, Angelegenheit. **brake:** Dickicht, Unterholz. 11 **fretty:** gitterförmig verziert (von *to fret*). **chervil:** Kerbel. 12 **to strain:** sich abmühen. 13 **to breed:** erzeugen, hervorbringen.

The Windhover

To Christ our Lord

I caught this morning morning's minion, king-
dom of daylight's dauphin, dapple-dawn-drawn Falcon, in his riding
Of the rolling level underneath him steady air, and striding
High there, how he rung upon the rein of a wimpling wing
In his ecstasy! then off, off forth on swing,
As a skate's heel sweeps smooth on a bow-bend: the hurl and gliding
Rebuffed the big wind. My heart in hiding
Stirred for a bird, – the achieve of, the mastery of the thing!

Brute beauty and valour and act, oh, air, pride, plume, here
Buckle! AND the fire that breaks from thee then, a billion
Times told lovelier, more dangerous, O my chevalier!

No wonder of it: shéer plód makes plough down sillion
Shine, and blue-bleak embers, ah my dear,
Fall, gall themselves, and gash gold-vermilion.

(c. 1877)

[Titel] **windhover:** Turmfalke. Die Widmung wurde dem Gedicht erst 1883 beigegeben. 1 **minion:** Günstling, Liebling. 2 **dauphin:** Königssohn, Erbprinz. **dapple-dawn-drawn Falcon:** etwa: von der Morgendämmerung angezogener gescheckter Falke (*dapple:* vermutl. selbständiges Attribut zu *falcon*; vgl. *dappled* ›gescheckt‹). 3 **to stride:** die Lüfte wie ein Reiter beherrschen. 4 **to ring:** spiralförmig ansteigen. **wimpling:** schwingend. 5 **swing:** Schwung. 6 **skate's heel:** vermutl.: Schlittschuhschneide (*heel:* Neigung). **to sweep:** gleiten. **bend:** Kurve, Krümmung. **hurl:** Schleudern, Wirbel. 7 **to rebuff:** zurückdrängen. 8 **to stir:** in Erregung geraten. **achieve:** Vollendung. 9 **brute:** tierisch. **valour:** Tapferkeit, Mut. **air:** Aussehen, Auftreten, Art. **plume:** Gefieder. 10 **to buckle: 1.** sich rüsten, wappnen; **2.** niederstürzen. 11 **told:** erachtet. **chevalier:** Ritter. 12 f. **sheer plod makes … shine:** reine Mühsal lässt den Pflug, der die Ackerfurche entlang geführt wird, erglänzen. 13 **blue-bleak:** blau-öde. **embers** (pl.): Asche. 14 **to gall:** wund reiben. **to gash:** etwa: leuchtend aufplatzen. **gold-vermilion:** goldrot.

Felix Randal

Felix Randal the farrier, O he is dead then? my duty all ended,
Who have watched his mould of man, big-boned and hardy-handsome
Pining, pining, till time when reason rambled in it and some
Fatal four disorders, fleshed there, all contended?

Sickness broke him. Impatient, he cursed at first, but mended
Being anointed and all; though a heavenlier heart began some
Months earlier, since I had our sweet reprieve and ransom
Tendered to him. Ah well, God rest him all road ever he offended!

This seeing the sick endears them to us, us too it endears.
My tongue had taught thee comfort, touch had quenched thy tears,
Thy tears had touched my heart, child, Felix, poor Felix Randal;

How far from then forethought of, all thy more boisterous years,
When thou at the random grim forge, powerful amidst peers,
Didst fettle for the great grey drayhorse his bright and battering sandal!

(c. 1880)

1 **farrier:** Hufschmied. 2 **mould:** Form; Gussform. **hardy:** robust. 3 **to pine:** langsam unter Schmerzen sterben. **to ramble:** umherschweifen; (im Delirium) unzusammenhängend reden. 4 **disorder:** Krankheit. **fleshed:** Fleisch geworden, eingefleischt. **to contend:** kämpfen. 5 **to mend:** sich bessern. 6 **to anoint s.o.:** jdm. die Krankensalbung spenden. 7 **reprieve and ransom:** Rettung und Erlösung (Hl. Altarsakrament). 8 **to tender:** darreichen. **all road ever he offended:** etwa: wie auch immer er gefehlt hat. 9 **to endear s.o.:** jdn. lieb und teuer machen. 10 **to quench:** stillen. 12 **forethought:** Vorbedacht. **boisterous:** ungestüm. 13 **random:** grob gemauert. **forge:** Esse. **peer:** Gefährte. 14 **to fettle:** anfertigen. **drayhorse:** Zugpferd. **to batter:** heftig schlagen.

Thoughts in Separation

We never meet; yet we meet day by day
   Upon those hills of life, dim and immense –
   The good we love, and sleep, our innocence.
O hills of life, high hills! And, higher than they,
Our guardian spirits meet at prayer and play.
   Beyond pain, joy, and hope, and long suspense,
   Above the summits of our souls, far hence,
An angel meets an angel on the way.

Beyond all good I ever believed of thee
   Or thou of me, these always love and live.
And though I fail of thy ideal of me,
My angel falls not short. They greet each other.
   Who knows, they may exchange the kiss we give,
Thou to thy crucifix, I to my mother.

(publ. 1875)

6 **suspense:** Ungewissheit, Zweifel. 7 **summit:** Gipfel, Höhepunkt.

Leda and the Swan

A sudden blow: the great wings beating still
Above the staggering girl, her thighs caressed
By the dark webs, her nape caught in his bill,
He holds her helpless breast upon his breast.

How can those terrified vague fingers push
The feathered glory from her loosening thighs?
And how can body, laid in that white rush,
But feel the strange heart beating where it lies?

A shudder in the loins engenders there
The broken wall, the burning roof and tower
And Agamemnon dead.
Being so caught up,
So mastered by the brute blood of the air,
Did she put on his knowledge with his power
Before the indifferent beak could let her drop?

(c. 1923)

[Titel] **Leda:** Gattin des Spartanerkönigs Tyndareos; Zeus näherte sich ihr in Schwanengestalt und zeugte Helena und Polydeukes. 2 **to stagger:** taumeln. **thigh:** (Ober-)Schenkel. **to caress:** liebkosen. 3 **web:** Schwimmhaut. **nape:** Nacken. **bill:** Schnabel. 5 **terrified:** entsetzt. 7 **rush:** Sturm. 9 **loins:** Lenden. **to engender:** zeugen. 10 Anspielung auf den Trojanischen Krieg. 11 **Agamemnon dead:** Nach seiner Rückkehr aus dem Trojanischen Krieg wurde Agamemnon von Klytämnestra und ihrem Liebhaber Ägisthus ermordet. **caught up:** ergriffen. 12 **brute:** tierisch. 14 **indifferent:** gleichgültig. **beak:** Schnabel.

Anthem for Doomed Youth

What passing-bells for these who die as cattle?
– Only the monstrous anger of the guns.
Only the stuttering rifles' rapid rattle
Can patter out their hasty orisons.
No mockeries now for them; no prayers nor bells;
Nor any voice of mourning save the choirs, –
The shrill, demented choirs of wailing shells;
And bugles calling for them from sad shires.

What candles may be held to speed them all?
Not in the hands of boys, but in their eyes
Shall shine the holy glimmers of goodbyes.
The pallor of girls' brows shall be their pall;
Their flowers the tenderness of patient minds,
And each slow dusk a drawing-down of blinds.

(c. 1917)

[Titel] **anthem:** Hymne. **doomed:** verloren, dem Untergang geweiht. 1 **passing-bells:** Sterbeglocken. 4 **to patter out:** herunterleiern. **orison:** Gebet. 5 **mockery:** Spott, Verhöhnung. 6 **to mourn:** trauern, klagen. 7 **demented:** irre, verrückt. **to wail:** wehklagen, jammern. **shell:** Granate. 8 **bugle:** Hornsignal. **shire:** Grafschaft. 9 **to speed s.o.:** jdm. beistehen. 12 **pallor:** Blässe. **brow:** Gesicht. **pall:** Leichen-, Sargtuch. 14 **dusk:** Abenddämmerung. **blind:** Vorhang; Jalousie.

The Serf

His naked skin clothed in the torrid mist
That puffs in smoke around the patient hooves,
The ploughman drives, a slow somnambulist,
And through the green his crimson furrow grooves.
His heart, more deeply than he wounds the plain,
Long by the rasping share of insult torn,
Red clod, to which the war-cry once was rain
And tribal spears the fatal sheaves of corn,
Lies fallow now. But as the turf divides
I see in the slow progress of his strides
Over the toppled clods and falling flowers,
The timeless, surly patience of the serf
That moves the nearest to the naked earth
And ploughs down palaces, and thrones, and towers.

(c. 1926)

[Titel] **serf:** Leibeigener; gemeint ist ein Zulu-Krieger, der im Dienst der Weißen steht. 1 **torrid:** brennend, glühend. 3 **somnambulist:** Schlafwandler. 4 **crimson:** purpur-, blutrot. **furrow:** Furche. **to groove:** (Furche) ziehen. 7 **clod:** Erdklumpen, Scholle. 8 **tribal:** Stammes-. **sheave:** Garbe. 9 **fallow:** brach. **turf:** Grasnabe. 10 **stride:** langer Schritt. 11 **to topple:** kippen. 12 **surly:** mürrisch, grob.

Luis de Camões

Camões, alone, of all the lyric race,
Born in the black aurora of disaster,
Can look a common soldier in the face:
I find a comrade where I sought a master:
For daily, while the stinking crocodiles
Glide from the mangroves on the swampy shore,
He shares my awning on the dhow, he smiles,
And tells me that he lived it all before.
Through fire and shipwreck, pestilence and loss,
Led by the ignis fatuus of duty
To a dog's death – yet of his sorrows king –
He shouldered high his voluntary Cross,
Wrestled his hardships into forms of beauty,
And taught his gorgon destinies to sing.

(c. 1944)

[Titel] **Luis de Camões:** Luís Vaz de Camões (um 1524–80), Verfasser des portugiesischen Nationalepos *Os Lusíadas.* 2 **aurora:** Morgenröte. 6 **swampy:** sumpfig. 7 **awning:** Sonnensegel. **dhow:** ostafrikanisches Küstensegelschiff mit Dreiecksegeln. 9 **pestilence:** Pest, Seuche. 10 **ignis fatuus** (Lat.): Irrlicht; Trugbild. 12 **voluntary:** freiwillig. 13 **to wrestle:** ringen. 14 **gorgon:** gorgonenhaft (die Gorgo-Medusa der griechischen Mythologie lässt ihre Betrachter zu Stein erstarren). **destiny:** Schicksal.

Who's Who

A shilling life will give you all the facts:
How Father beat him, how he ran away,
What were the struggles of his youth, what acts
Made him the greatest figure of his day:
Of how he fought, fished, hunted, worked all night,
Though giddy, climbed new mountains; named a sea:
Some of the last researchers even write
Love made him weep his pints like you and me.

With all his honours on, he sighed for one
Who, say astonished critics, lived at home;
Did little jobs about the house with skill
And nothing else; could whistle; would sit still
Or potter round the garden; answered some
Of his long marvellous letters but kept none.

(c. 1934)

[Titel] **Who's Who:** Lexikon über Personen des öffentlichen Lebens. 1 **shilling life:** kurze, preisgünstige Lebensgeschichte. 6 **giddy:** schwindelig. 7 **researcher:** Forscher. 8 **pint:** Schoppen. 9 **to sigh for s.o.:** sich nach jdm. sehnen. 13 **to potter:** herumhantieren.

As evening fell the day's oppression lifted;
Tall peaks came into focus; it had rained:
Across wide lawns and cultured flowers drifted
The conversation of the highly trained.

Thin gardeners watched them pass and priced their shoes;
A chauffeur waited, reading in the drive,
For them to finish their exchange of views:
It looked a picture of the way to live.

Far off, no matter what good they intended,
Two armies waited for a verbal error
With well-made implements for causing pain,

And on the issue of their charm depended
A land laid waste with all its young men slain,
Its women weeping, and its towns in terror.

(*Sonnets from China* XV) (c. 1938)

1 **oppression:** Druck; Beklemmung. 2 **focus:** Brennpunkt. 3 **to drift:** treiben. 5 **to price s.th.:** den Preis von etwas schätzen. 6 **drive:** Fahrweg, Auffahrt. 11 **implement:** Vorrichtung, Werkzeug. 12 **issue:** Ergebnis, Resultat. 13 **to lay s.th. waste:** etwas verwüsten, verheeren.

GEORGE BARKER

Sonnet of Fishes

Bright drips the morning from its trophied nets
Looped along a sky flickering fish and wing,
Cobbles like salmon crowd up waterfalling
Streets where life dies thrashing as the sea forgets,
True widow, what she has lost; and, ravished, lets
The knuckledustered sun shake bullying
A fist of glory over her. Every thing,
Even the sly night, gives up its lunar secrets.

And I with pilchards cold in my pocket make
Red-eyed a way to the bed. But in my blood
Crying I hear, still, the leap of the silver diver
Caught in four cords after his fatal strake:
And then, the immense imminence not understood,
Death, in a dark, in a deep, in a dream, for ever.

(publ. 1950)

1 **trophied:** mit Trophäen geschmückt. 2 **to loop:** schlingen. **to flicker:** flackern; flattern. 3 **cobbles** (pl.): Kopfsteinpflaster. **salmon:** Lachs. 4 **to thrash:** um sich schlagen. 5 **to ravish:** schänden, vergewaltigen; entzücken. 6 **knuckledustered:** mit Schlagring versehen. **to bully:** tyrannisieren, einschüchtern. 8 **sly:** verschlagen. **lunar:** Mond-. 9 **pilchard:** Sardine. 12 **cord:** Strick, Leine. **strake:** Plankengang. 13 **imminence:** drohende Gefahr. 14 **dark / deep:** Dunkelheit, Tiefe.

I Am the Great Sun

From a Normandy crucifix of 1632

I am the great sun, but you do not see me,
I am your husband, but you turn away.
I am the captive, but you do not free me,
I am the captain you will not obey.

I am the truth, but you will not believe me,
I am the city where you will not stay,
I am your wife, your child, but you will leave me,
I am that God to whom you will not pray.

I am your counsel, but you do not hear me,
I am the lover whom you will betray.
I am the victor, but you do not cheer me,
I am the holy dove whom you will slay.

I am your life, but if you will not name me,
Seal up your soul with tears, and never blame me.

(c. 1955)

3 **captive:** Gefangener. 9 **counsel:** Rat; Rechtsberater. 10 **to betray:** verraten. 11 **victor:** Sieger. **to cheer:** zujubeln. 12 **dove:** Taube. **to slay:** erschlagen. 13 f. Vgl. Mt. 10,32 f. 14 **to seal up:** versiegeln.

The Card-Players

Jan van Hogspeuw staggers to the door
And pisses at the dark. Outside, the rain
Courses in cart-ruts down the deep mud lane.
Inside, Dirk Dogstoerd pours himself some more,
And holds a cinder to his clay with tongs,
Belching out smoke. Old Prijck snores with the gale,
His skull face firelit; someone behind drinks ale,
And opens mussels, and croaks scraps of songs
Towards the ham-hung rafters about love.
Dirk deals the cards. Wet century-wide trees
Clash in surrounding starlessness above
This lamplit cave, where Jan turns back and farts,
Gobs at the grate, and hits the queen of hearts.

Rain, wind and fire! The secret, bestial peace!

(c. 1970)

1 **to stagger:** taumeln, schwanken. 3 **to course:** rinnen. **cart-ruts:** Karrenfurchen. 5 **cinder:** ausgeglühte Kohle. **clay:** Tonpfeife. 6 **to belch:** rülpsen. **to snore:** schnarchen. **gale:** Sturm. 7 **skull:** Schädel. 8 **to croak:** krächzen. 9 **ham-hung:** mit Schinken behangen. **rafter:** Dachsparren. 11 **to clash:** aneinander stoßen. 13 **to gob:** (aus)spucken. **grate:** Feuerrost, Kamin.

I dreamt we slept in a moss in Donegal
On turf banks under blankets, with our faces
Exposed all night in a wetting drizzle,
Pallid as the dripping sapling birches.
Lorenzo and Jessica in a cold climate.
Diarmuid and Grainne waiting to be found.
Darkly asperged and censed, we were laid out
Like breathing effigies on a raised ground.
And in that dream I dreamt – how like you this? –
Our first night years ago in that hotel
When you came with your deliberate kiss
To raise us towards the lovely and painful
Covenants of flesh; our separateness;
The respite in our dewy dreaming faces.

(*Glanmore Sonnets* X) (publ. 1975)

1 **moss:** Torfmoor. **Donegal:** Grafschaft im Nordwesten Irlands. 2 **turf bank:** Erhebung im Torfmoor. **drizzle:** Sprühregen. 4 **pallid:** bleich. **sapling birch:** junge Birke (*sapling:* Schössling). 5 f. **Lorenzo and Jessica ... Diarmuid and Grainne:** flüchtige Liebespaare aus Shakespeares *Merchant of Venice* bzw. der keltischen Mythologie. 7 **to asperge s.th.:** etwas (mit Weihwasser) besprengen. **to cense s.th.:** etwas beweihräuchern. **to lay s.o. out:** jdn. aufbahren. 8 **effigy:** Bild, Abbild. 9 **how like you this:** Zitat aus Wyatts Liebesklage »They flee from me«, Z. 14. 11 **deliberate:** wohlerwogen. 13 **covenant:** Bündnis. 14 **respite:** Aufschub; Ruhepause.

Editorische Notiz

Das Glossar erklärt in der Regel alle Wörter, die nicht in *Reclams Englischem Wörterbuch* von Dieter Hamblock (Stuttgart: Reclam, 1996) verzeichnet sind. Die Sonette sind unabhängig voneinander glossiert.

Bei den älteren Texten wurden Orthographie und Interpunktion abweichend von der jeweiligen Quellen-Edition behutsam modernisiert. Außerdem wurde die Typographie der Sonette von Wyatt bis Daniel – mit Ausnahme von Sidney – vereinheitlicht.

Im Glossar verwendete Abkürzungen

adv.	adverb
Lat.	Latin
pl.	plural
s.o.	someone
s.th.	something

Zu den Autoren und Gedichten

W. H. AUDEN

21. 2. 1907 York – 29. 9. 1973 Wien

Wystan Hugh Auden, als Sohn eines Arztes geboren, studierte Politik, Philosophie und englische Literatur am Christ Church College in Oxford (1925–28), wo sich eine Gruppe linksgerichteter Lyriker (MacNeice, Spender, Day Lewis) um ihn scharte, die er stark beeinflusste. 1928/29 lebte er in Berlin und arbeitete dann als Lehrer an verschiedenen Schulen in England (1929–35), bevor ihn Reisen nach Island (1936), Spanien (1937), China, Japan und in die Vereinigten Staaten (1938) führten. Anfang 1939 ließ er sich in New York nieder, wirkte als Universitätsdozent (1940–50) und erwarb 1946 die amerikanische Staatsbürgerschaft. 1948–57 hielt er sich abwechselnd in New York und Italien auf, später in Kirchstetten (bei Wien) und Oxford. Er erhielt zahlreiche Auszeichnungen und war von 1956–61 Professor für Dichtkunst in Oxford.

Obwohl Auden auch als Dramatiker, Essayist, Übersetzer und Librettist hervorgetreten ist, beruht sein Ruhm auf seiner Vielseitigkeit als Lyriker. Kein zweiter englischer Dichter beherrscht eine solche Fülle lyrischer Genres, Vers- und Strophenformen. Die wichtigsten Vorbilder hat er selbst in seinem späten Gedicht »A Thanksgiving« (1973) genannt: Horaz, Goethe, Hardy, Yeats, Frost, Graves, Rilke und Brecht. Doch fügte er die verschiedenartigen Einflüsse seinem völlig unverwechselbaren Idiom ein, so dass er seinerseits zum Vorbild für jüngere Dichter werden konnte. »No other poet of his generation can place beside his a body of work so exciting for its peculiar insight, its range of reference, and its skill in the use of language and rhythm« (Kenneth Allott).

Audens Sonette sind am englischen Typus orientiert und finden sich hauptsächlich in zwei Zyklen, von denen der eine (*In Time of War*, 1938, später u. d. T. *Sonnets from China*) während des chinesisch-japanischen Krieges, der andere (*The Quest*, 1940) während des Zweiten Weltkriegs in den Vereinigten Staaten entstand. Im Sonett treten Audens Stilmerkmale klar hervor, vor allem die Kunst der lakonisch-abstrakten Formulierung und der Hang zum *understatement.*

Wichtigste Lyrikbände: *Poems* (1930, erw. 1933); *Look, Stranger!* (1936); *Letters from Iceland* (zus. mit Louis MacNeice, 1937); *Journey to a War* (zus. mit Christopher Isherwood, 1939); *Another Time* (1940); *New Year Letter* (1941); *For the Time Being* (1944); *The Age of Anxiety* (1947); *Collected Shorter Poems 1930–1944* (1950); *Nones* (1951); *The Shield of Achilles* (1955); *Homage to Clio* (1960); *About the House* (1965); *Collected Shorter Poems 1927–1957* (1966); *Collected Longer Poems* (1968); *City without Walls* (1969); *Academic Graffiti* (1971); *Epistle to a Godson* (1972). – (Postum) *Thank You, Fog* (1974); *Collected Poems,* hrsg. von Edward Mendelson (1976).

Text: W. H. Auden, *Collected Poems,* hrsg. von Edward Mendelson, London: Faber and Faber, [2]1991. Reprinted by permission of Faber and Faber Ltd., London.

Sekundärliteratur: Peter Krahé, »Nachrufpersönlichkeiten: Ein Vergleich von Audens ›Who's Who‹ und Benns ›Fürst Kraft‹«, in: *Sprachkunst* 16 (1985) S. 246–255; John Williams, *Reading Poetry: A Contextual Introduction*, London 1985, S. 21–23 [zu »As evening fell«].

GEORGE BARKER

26. 2. 1913 Loughton (Essex) – 27. 10. 1991 Itteringham (Norfolk)

George Barker wuchs als Sohn eines englischen Polizisten und einer irischen Mutter in einem Londoner Arbeiterviertel auf und wurde katholisch erzogen. Schon mit siebzehn Jahren publizierte er seine ersten Gedichte und galt neben seinem Freund Dylan Thomas bald als führender Dichter der vierziger Jahre. 1935 heiratete er, unterhielt aber zahlreiche außereheliche Beziehungen, darunter mit der kanadischen Autorin Elizabeth Smart. 1939 lehrte er als Professor für Dichtkunst in Japan, 1940–44 fand er als Literaturkritiker in den Vereinigten Staaten sein Auskommen und kehrte dann nach England zurück. 1951–56 wohnte er abwechselnd in London und Barcelona, seit 1957 auch wieder in den Vereinigten Staaten. 1960 entdeckte er seine Liebe für Italien, wo ihn das disziplinierende Vorbild von Horaz und Catull zu einigen seiner besten Gedichte anregte. Die geschliffene Diktion und der ironische Unterton der seit 1960 entstandenen freien Verse führten ihn in die Nähe rhythmisierter Prosa. Seine letzten zwanzig Lebensjahre verbrachte er mit Elspeth Langlands, der Mutter seiner fünf jüngsten Kinder, in Itteringham, nördlich von Norwich.

Barker wurde von der mittelenglischen Lyrik ebenso beeinflusst wie von Villon, Donne, Blake, Byron, Tennyson, Hopkins und Housman. Sein umfangreiches Werk umfasst neben religiöser und erotischer Lyrik auch Balladen, Naturgedichte, Verssatiren, Hochzeits-, Huldigungs-, Meditations- und Kindergedichte, fand jedoch nicht immer gebührende Anerkennung. So hatte die offenherzige Erotik seiner Versautobiographie *The True Confession of George Barker* (1950) nach der Erstsendung durch die BBC einen Presseskandal sowie ein parlamentarisches Nachspiel zur Folge, und der Faber-Verlag verweigerte sogar die Publikation des Werkes. Auch später wartete Barker immer wieder mit einer seinem häretischen Katholizismus entspringenden Mischung von religiösen und sexuellen Motiven auf. Kenneth Allott hat ihn zutreffend als einen »hit-or-miss artist« charakterisiert. Doch auch wenn seine Lyrik – wie die von Donne – gelegentlich sensationslüstern, obskur und mit einem Schuss theatralischer Rhetorik versetzt ist, so hat Yeats ihm nicht ohne Grund Subtilität und einen Sinn für fein abgestufte rhythmische Nuancen bescheinigt.

Wichtigste Lyrikbände: *Thirty Preliminary Poems* (1933); *Poems* (1935); *Calamiterror* (1937); *Lament and Triumph* (1940); *Selected Poems* (1941); *Eros in Dogma* (1944); *The True Confession of George Barker* (1950, erw. 1964); *News of the World* (1950); *A Vision of Beasts and Gods* (1954); *Collected Poems 1930–1955* (1957); *The View from a Blind I* (1962); *Dreams of a Summer Night* (1966); *The Golden Chains* (1968); *Poems of Places and People* (1971); *In Memory of David Archer* (1973); *Dialogues etc.* (1976); *Villa Stellar* (1978); *Anno Domini* (1983); *Collected Poems,* hrsg. von Robert Fraser (1987). – (Postum) *Street Ballads* (1992).

Text: George Barker, *Collected Poems,* hrsg. von Robert Fraser, London: Faber and Faber, 1987. Reprinted by permission of Faber and Faber Ltd., London.

Sekundärliteratur: Martha Fodaski, *George Barker,* New York 1969 [nicht zu »Sonnet of Fishes«].

ELIZABETH BARRETT BROWNING

6. 3. 1806 Coxhoe Hall (Durham) – 29. 6. 1861 Florenz

Elizabeth Barrett verbrachte Kindheit und Jugend auf dem Anwesen ihres Vaters in Hertfordshire, der als ehemaliger Sklavenhändler ein strenges Regiment führte. Schon als Kind erwarb sie eine so umfassende Bildung, dass sie mit acht Jahren Homer im Original lesen konnte. Später beherrschte sie neben Griechisch, Latein und Hebräisch auch die wichtigsten modernen Sprachen. Zwei frühe Schicksalsschläge verstärkten eine angeborene Neigung zur Melancholie. Mit fünfzehn Jahren zog sie sich bei einem Sturz vom Pferd eine Rückgratverletzung zu und blieb jahrelang ans Bett gefesselt, dann löste der Tod des Bruders eine seelische Krise aus. Mit Gedichten und Essays gewann sie die Anerkennung literarisch interessierter Kreise, darunter die des sechs Jahre jüngeren Robert Browning. Die heimliche Heirat mit ihm im Jahre 1846 und die gemeinsame Flucht nach Florenz führten zur Genesung. Elizabeth Barrett Browning sympathisierte dort mit dem Freiheitswillen der Italiener und zeigte in ihrer Lyrik ein zunehmendes Interesse an sozialen Problemen.

Die *Sonnets from the Portuguese* (1845/46) variieren petrakistische Konventionen aus weiblicher Sicht und sind an ihren »little Portuguese« Robert Browning gerichtet. Das enorme Ansehen, das der Zyklus zu Lebzeiten der Autorin genoss, ist inzwischen verflogen. Kaum noch jemand teilt die Überzeugung ihres Ehemannes, es handle sich um die bedeutendsten englischen Sonette seit Shakespeare, oder Poes Auffassung, Elizabeth Barrett Browning habe all ihre dichtenden Zeitgenossen – männlich oder weiblich – überflügelt. Stattdessen meint Patrick Cruttwell, dass stilistische Gewandtheit weder für das konventionelle Thema (aufrichtige Liebe) noch für die antiquierte Sprache zu entschädigen vermöge. Bedenkt man aber, wie begeistert sich G. K. Chesterton geäußert hat, so fragt sich doch, ob das letzte Wort über sie tatsächlich schon gesprochen ist: »With her reappeared in poetry a certain element which had not been present in it since the last days of Elizabethan literature, the fusion of the most elementary human passion with something which can only be described as wit.« Auch der junge Rilke war von der Autorin angetan: die stilistische Eleganz der *Sonnets* veranlasste ihn, den Zyklus 1908 ins Deutsche zu übertragen.

Text: Elizabeth Barrett Browning, *The Complete Works,* Bd. 3, hrsg. von Charlotte Porter und Helen A. Clarke, New York: AMS Press, 1973.

Sekundärliteratur: Ruth Freifrau v. Ledebur, »›If thou must love me‹«, in: Reinhold Schiffer / Hermann J. Weiand (Hrsg.), *Insight III: Analyses of English and American Poetry,* Frankfurt a. M. 1969, S. 50–53; Dorothy Mermin, »The Female Poet and the Embarrassed Reader: Elizabeth Barrett Browning's *Sonnets from the Portuguese*«, in: *Journal of English Literary History* 48 (1981) S. 351–367.

ROY CAMPBELL

2. 10. 1901 Durban (Südafrika) – 23. 4. 1957 bei Setúbal (Portugal)

Roy Campbell, als Sohn eines Arztes geboren, verbrachte Kindheit und Jugend in der idyllischen Umgebung seiner Heimatstadt Durban und in Rhodesien. 1918 reiste er nach Oxford, um englische Literatur zu studieren, und freundete sich mit dem gleichaltrigen Komponisten William Walton an, der ihn in die *high society* der modernen englischen Literatur einführte (Edith Sitwell, T. S. Eliot, Wyndham Lewis). Er brach sein Studium ab und trampte in Frankreich umher, wo er sich für Baudelaire, Rimbaud und Valéry begeisterte. 1922 heiratete er in London und kehrte nach dem sensationellen Erfolg von *The Flaming Terrapin* (1924) nach Südafrika zurück, wo er mit William Plomer und Laurens van der Post die Zeitschrift *Voorslag* (1926) herausgab. Doch seine heftige Kritik an der Kultur- und Rassenpolitik der Kapprovinz trieb ihn bald in die Isolation, so dass er sich gezwungen sah, der Heimat endgültig den Rücken zu kehren. 1927 ließ er sich mit seiner Frau und den beiden Töchtern in Kent nieder und arbeitete als Literaturkritiker. 1928–33 lebte er als Fischer in der Provence, 1933–36 als Pferdehändler in Toledo, bis ihn der hautnah erlebte Spanische Bürgerkrieg von dort vertrieb. Als Konvertit sympathisierte er mit Franco und kehrte 1938 nach Toledo zurück. 1942–45 diente er als britischer Soldat u. a. in Ostafrika. Nach dem Krieg leitete er in London die Literaturabteilung der BBC (1946–49) und wirkte als Mitherausgeber der Zeitschrift *Catacomb* (1949–51). 1952 ließ er sich in Portugal nieder und unternahm von dort aus Vortragsreisen in die Vereinigten Staaten, nach Kanada und Südafrika. 1957 kam er bei einem Autounfall in der Nähe von Lissabon ums Leben.

In seinen besten Gedichten verbindet Campbell das technische und rhetorische Geschick von Dryden, Pope und Byron mit der melodischen Sinnlichkeit der französischen Symbolisten. Das zeigen auch seine Sonette, deren Glanzlichter wie eine poetische Lebensbeschreibung en miniature anmuten: »The Zebras« (1925), »The Serf« (1926), »Wings« (1930), »The Road to Arles« (1933), »Toledo, July 1936« (1936), »San Juan de la Cruz« (1942) und »Luis de Camões« (1944). Neben zwei Autobiographien und der kritischen Studie *Lorca* (1952) verdienen seine zahlreichen Vers- und Prosaübersetzungen aus den romanischen Sprachen Beachtung. Dylan Thomas nannte ihn »a poet of genius«, und Charles Causley schrieb: »At his best he produced a body of lyric poems among the finest of those written in English.«

Wichtigste Lyrikbände: *The Flaming Terrapin* (1924); *The Wayzgoose* (1928); *Adamastor* (1930); *The Georgiad* (1931); *Flowering Reeds* (1933); *Mithraic Emblems* (1936); *Flowering Rifle* (1939, rev. 1957); *Talking Bronco* (1946); *Collected Poems* (1949). – (Postum) *Collected Poems,* Bd. 2 (1957); *Collected Poems,* Bd. 3 (1960; Übersetzungen).

Text: Roy Campbell, *Collected Works*, hrsg. von Peter Alexander, Michael Chapman und Marcia Leveson, Bd. 1: *Poetry*, Craighell: Ad Donker Publishers, 1985. Abdruck nach: Roy Campbell, *Collected Poems*, London: The Bodley Head, 1949. Reprinted by permission of Jonathan Ball Publishers (Pty) Ltd., Johannesburg.

Sekundärliteratur: Peter Alexander, *Roy Campbell: A Critical Biography,* Oxford 1982, S. 64 f. [zu »The Serf«]; Michael Hanke, »Roy Campbell: ›Luis de Camões‹«, in: M. H. (Hrsg.), *Englische Gedichte des 20. Jahrhunderts: Interpretationen*, Stuttgart 1997, S. 153–159; ders., »Afrikanische Apokalypse: Roy Campbells Sonett ›The Serf‹«, in: *Literatur in Wissenschaft und Unterricht* (im Druck); John Povey, *Roy Campbell*, Boston 1977, S. 59–62 [zu »The Serf«].

CHARLES CAUSLEY

* 24. 8. 1917 Launceston (Cornwall)

Charles Causley ist das einzige Kind einer Arbeiterfamilie. Der Vater – Soldat im Ersten Weltkrieg – starb 1924 an den Folgen eines deutschen Giftgasangriffs. Nach dem Schulbesuch arbeitete Causley bei einem Bauunternehmer und im Elektrizitätswerk seiner Heimatstadt (1933–40). Von seinem Kriegsdienst in der Royal Navy (1940–46), der Lehrerausbildung am Peterborough Training College (1946) und zahlreichen späteren Auslandsaufenthalten abgesehen, hat er sein ganzes Leben in Launceston verbracht, wo er von 1947 bis 1976 als Volksschullehrer (»thirty years in chalk Siberias«), daneben auch als freier Mitarbeiter der BBC und Herausgeber zahlreicher Anthologien wirkte. Er wurde für seine Lyrik mehrfach ausgezeichnet, zuletzt mit dem Heywood Hill Prize (2000).

Der Zweite Weltkrieg ließ ihn zum Dichter reifen: »As well as the inevitable wartime subjects of separation, love, death in far and lonely places, I have also been obsessed by the theme of lost innocence.« Als entscheidende frühe Einflüsse nennt er die Dichter des Ersten Weltkriegs (Sassoon, Owen, Blunden) und die Dichter um Auden. Eine weitere wichtige Inspirationsquelle ist seine Heimat Cornwall. Unbekümmert um Moden, hat er sich keiner der literarischen Gruppierungen des letzten halben Jahrhunderts angeschlossen. Freie Verse handhabt er mit dem gleichen Geschick wie die traditionelle Metrik, das Sonett ebenso wie die lange und kurze Verserzählung für Kinder. Vor allem ist er ein Meister der Balladenform. Weniger Beachtung haben seine reizvollen Kurzgeschichten (*Hands to Dance,* 1951) und Versdramen (darunter *The Ballad of Aucassin and Nicolette,* 1981) gefunden. Anlässlich seines 80. Geburtstags ehrte ihn der damalige *poeta laureatus* Ted Hughes als »this marvellously resourceful, original poet, yet among all known poets the only one who could be called a man of the people, in the old, best sense«.

In seinem bekanntesten Gedicht, der Christusklage »I Am the Great Sun« (1955), perfektioniert Causley eine Repetitionstechnik, die auf mittelalterliche Vorbilder verweist. Mit Blick auf dieses Sonett wird er oft als christlicher Autor bezeichnet, eine Einschätzung, die durch das gleichzeitig entstandene Seitenstück »At the British War Cemetery, Bayeux« relativiert wird. Er selbst sagt von sich: »I'm not absolutely sure about my position as a religious poet, though some people call me that.«

Wichtigste Lyrikbände: *Farewell, Aggie Weston* (1951); *Survivor's Leave* (1953); *Union Street* (1957); *Johnny Alleluia* (1961); *Underneath the Water* (1968); *Figure of 8* (1969); *Figgie Hobbin* (1970); *Collected Poems 1951–1975* (1975); *Secret Destinations* (1984); *A Field of Vision* (1988); *Collected Poems for Children* (1996); *Collected Poems 1951–2000* (2000).

Text: Charles Causley, *Collected Poems 1951–2000*, London: Macmillan, 2000. Reprinted by permission of David Higham Associates Ltd., London.

Sekundärliteratur: Michael Hanke, »Christian Motifs in the Poetry of Charles Causley«, in: *Zeitschrift für Anglistik und Amerikanistik* 45 (1997) S. 197–207; Ewald Standop, *Aufsätze zur englischen Versdichtung: Von Chaucer bis Dylan Thomas*, Würzburg 1995, S. 119 f.; Ronald Tamplin, *Rhythm and Rhyme*, Buckingham 1993, S. 76–78.

JOHN CLARE

13. 7. 1793 Helpston (Northamptonshire) –
20. 5. 1864 Northampton

John Clare war Sohn eines Landarbeiters, der ihm eine rudimentäre Schulausbildung ermöglichte. Seine Laufbahn als Lyriker begann er unter dem Einfluss von James Thomsons Pastoraldichtung *The Seasons.* Keats' Verleger John Taylor wurde auf ihn aufmerksam und publizierte seine erste Sammlung *Poems Descriptive of Rural Life and Scenery* (1820) als Werk eines einfachen Bauerndichters (»peasant poet«). Damit wurde Clare schlagartig bekannt, doch schon der nächste Band *The Village Minstrel and Other Poems* (1821) war ein Misserfolg. Obwohl Lord Radstock ihn finanziell unterstützte (und sich dafür das Recht nahm, sozialkritische Passagen aus seiner Lyrik zu streichen), lebte der Dichter mit seiner Familie zeitlebens in Armut. Die finanziellen Schwierigkeiten führten zu geistiger Verwirrung, so dass er von 1837 bis zu seinem Tod in Heilanstalten leben musste, wobei jedoch seine schöpferische Kraft bis mindestens 1850 erhalten blieb. Kenner halten die in diesen Jahren entstandene Lyrik sogar für das Beste, was er geschrieben hat.

Wie »The Thrush's Nest« (1835) beweist, hatte Clare eine Vorliebe für die lockere, von Fragen nach formaler und gedanklicher

Gliederung unbelastete Sonettform. Als einer der bedeutendsten englischen Naturlyriker wurde er erst im 20. Jahrhundert entdeckt.

Text: John Clare, *The Poems,* Bd. 2, hrsg. von J. W. Tibble, London: Dent, 1935.

Sekundärliteratur: Hans Ulrich Seeber, »Einleitung« zu Teil I, in: Günter Ahrends / H. U. S. (Hrsg.), *Englische und amerikanische Naturdichtung im 20. Jahrhundert*, Tübingen 1985, S. 9–30, bes. S. 14–18.

SAMUEL DANIEL

1562 Taunton (Somerset) – Oktober 1619 Beckington (Wiltshire)

Samuel Daniel war Sohn eines Musiklehrers und begann 1579 ein Studium am Magdalen College in Oxford, das er jedoch 1582 abbrach. Diplomatische Aufträge führten ihn auf den Kontinent (Frankreich, Italien), bevor er die Erziehung des dritten Grafen Pembroke (eines Neffen von Sir Philip Sidney) und der Lady Anne Clifford übernahm. Als einer der produktivsten Autoren seiner Zeit schrieb er unermüdlich Pastoralstücke, Maskenspiele und Tragödien für das Hoftheater, kritische und historische Studien sowie ein achtbändiges, unvollendet gebliebenes Epos in Stanzen über die Rosenkriege 1455–85 (*The History of the Civil Wars between York and Lancaster,* 1595–1609). Bis kurz vor seinem Tode arbeitete er an einer Geschichte Englands. Von literarhistorischem Interesse ist sein Plädoyer für eine gereimte englische Versdichtung in *A Defence of Ryme* (1603), der Antwort auf Thomas Campions *The Art of English Poesy* (1602).

Von Daniels umfangreichem Werk haben nur eine Hand voll Sonette aus dem von Tasso und Desportes inspirierten *Delia*-Zyklus (1592) überlebt, darunter die Nummern 31 (»Look, Delia«), 33 (»When men shall find«), 42 (»Beauty, sweet love«), 45 (»Carecharmer sleep«) und 46 (»Let others sing of knights and palladines«). »They have a dignity of feeling and a natural flow and music which remind us of the more contemplative of Shakespeare's sonnets« (James Reeves).

Text: Samuel Daniel, *Poems and A Defence of Ryme,* hrsg. von Arthur Colby Sprague, Chicago: University of Chicago Press, 1965.

Sekundärliteratur: Diethild Bludau, »Sonettstruktur bei Samuel Daniel«, in: *Shakespeare Jahrbuch* 94 (1958) S. 63–89; Joan Rees, *Samuel Daniel: A Critical and Biographical Study*, Liverpool 1964, S. 13–34; C. F. Williamson, »The Design of Daniel's *Delia*«, in: *Review of English Studies* 19 (1968) S. 251–260.

JOHN DONNE

Januar oder Februar 1572 oder 1573 London – 31. 3. 1631 London

John Donne, der Erste und Größte der *metaphysical poets*, stammte aus einer wohlhabenden katholischen Kaufmannsfamilie. Nach dem Studium in Oxford und dem Besuch der Londoner Juristenschule Lincoln's Inn trat er in die Staatskirche ein und nahm 1596/1597 an Kaperfahrten nach Cádiz und zu den Azoren teil. Als ehemaliger Sekretär des Lordsiegelbewahrers Lord Egerton (1597/98) war er auf bestem Wege, Karriere zu machen, als er auf den Gedanken verfiel, heimlich dessen Nichte zu heiraten. Mit der Eheschließung 1601 zerschlugen sich alle Aussichten auf eine hohe Staatsstellung, doch der von ungezügeltem Ehrgeiz getriebene Donne machte sich Hoffnungen auf eine Zukunft in der Kirche. Auch wenn sich zwischen den Zeilen seiner religiösen Dichtung das nagende Gewissen des Renegaten meldet, dessen Bruder als Glaubenszeuge im Kerker gestorben war: Mit der Ernennung zum Dean von St. Paul's erreichte er 1621 den Gipfel seiner Laufbahn. Von der neuen Position aus ist er bemüht, einen scharfen Trennungsstrich zwischen dem jungen *libertin* Jack Donne, dem Verfasser gewagter erotischer Gedichte, und Dr. John Donne, dem wortgewaltigen und sittenstrengen Kanzelprediger, zu ziehen.

Schon manche Zeitgenossen lehnten Donne als schwierig und rau ab. Er selbst aber war sich seines Ranges durchaus bewusst und verteidigte seinen Stil: »I sing not, Siren-like, to tempt; for I / Am harsh.« Eine spätere Generation nahm Dr. Johnsons Auslassungen über die *metaphysical poets* zum Anlass, einen der bedeutendsten Renaissancedichter in der Versenkung verschwinden zu lassen; erst zu Beginn des 20. Jahrhunderts wird er wiederentdeckt und einem faszinierten Publikum vorgestellt. Donne ist ein Meister des *conceit,* der überraschenden, paradox wirkenden Metapher, die schlagartig Geistiges und Sinnliches, Nah- und Fernliegendes zusammenzwingt. Er beherrscht die Kunst des Registerwechsels und der Stilmischung wie außer ihm nur Shakespeare.

Neben Liebes- und Hochzeitsgedichten, Elegien, Epigrammen, Satiren und Versepisteln stehen geistliche Gedichte, darunter drei Hymnen, der Sonettzyklus *La Corona* (um 1607), den er seiner Mäzenin Magdalen Herbert – der Mutter George Herberts – gewidmet hat und seine neunzehn *Holy Sonnets* (1609), die 1945 von Benjamin Britten vertont wurden. »Witty, hugely versatile, paradoxical, passionate, his emotions spiced – often harshly – with sharp reason, Donne was – as he remains – a true original; and every word he wrote bears the mark of a personal truth that almost burns a hole on the page« (Charles Causley).

Text: John Donne, *The Complete English Poems,* hrsg. von A. J. Smith, Harmondsworth: Penguin, 1986.

Sekundärliteratur: Robert J. Blanch, »Fear and Despair in Donne's *Holy Sonnets*«, in: *American Benedictine Review* 25 (1974) S. 476–484; John Carey, *John Donne: Life, Mind and Art*, London 1981, S. 198–201 [zu *Holy Sonnets* X]; Roman Dubinski, »Donne's *Holy Sonnets* and the Seven Penitential Psalms«, in: *Renaissance and Reformation* 22 (1986) S. 201–216; Louis L. Martz, *The Poetry of Meditation: A Study in English Religious Literature*, New Haven [2]1962 ([1]1954), S. 50–52 [zu *Holy Sonnets* VII]; John V. Hagopian, »›Holy Sonnet 14‹«, in: Reinhold Schiffer / Hermann J. Weiand (Hrsg.), *Insight III: Analyses of English and American Poetry,* Frankfurt a. M. 1969, S. 88–96; Roger B. Rollin, »›Fantastique Ague‹: The *Holy Sonnets* and Religious Melancholy«, in: Claude J. Summers / Ted-Larry Pebworth (Hrsg.), *The Eagle and the Dove: Reassessing John Donne*, Columbia 1986, S. 131–146; R. V. Young, »Donne's *Holy Sonnets* and the Theology of Grace«, in: Claude J. Summers / Ted-Larry Pebworth (Hrsg.), *»Bright Shootes of Everlastingnesse«: The Seventeenth-Century Religious Lyric*, Columbia 1987, S. 20–39.

MICHAEL DRAYTON

1563 Hartshill (Warwickshire) – 23. 12. 1631 London

Michael Drayton gehörte als Sohn eines Handwerkers zu den wenigen Berufsdichtern seiner Zeit. Neben scharfen Kritikern fanden sich zu seinen Lebzeiten auch Bewunderer wie William Browne, der ihn als »zweiten Ovid« feierte. Sein ehrgeizigstes Werk, das gigantische topographische Epos *Polyolbion* (1612,

1622), ist inzwischen ebenso in Vergessenheit geraten wie seine historischen Gedichte *Gaveston* (1593), *Robert, Duke of Normandie* (1596), Versepisteln, Satiren, Eklogen und das Feenepos *Nymphidia* (1627). Nur die Ballade »The Battle of Agincourt« (1627) und eine Hand voll *anthology pieces* aus dem unentwegt umgearbeiteten Sonettzyklus *Ideas Mirrour* (1594) sichern ihm auch heute noch dichterisches Ansehen. Thema von Draytons Sonettzyklus ist – wie schon die Verwendung eines platonischen Schlüsselbegriffs als Titel zeigt – die geistige Sublimierung der Liebe. Das mit Abstand und mit Recht berühmteste Gedicht daraus ist »Since there's no help, come let us kiss and part«, ein klassisches Beispiel für die Möglichkeit des englischen Sonetts, mit einem pointierten *couplet* die in den Quartetten exponierte Situation auf den Kopf zu stellen. »One cannot ask more of fourteen lines« (C. S. Lewis).

Text: Michael Drayton, *The Works,* Bd. 2, hrsg. von William Hebel, Oxford: Shakespeare Head Press, 1941.

Sekundärliteratur: Hans Combecher, *Deutung englischer Gedichte,* Bd. 2, Frankfurt a. M. 1965, S. 42–44; Reimer Jehmlich, *Die Bildlichkeit in der Liebeslyrik Sir Philip Sidneys, Michael Draytons und John Donnes (»Astrophel and Stella«, »Idea«, »Songs and Sonets«)*, Diss. Kiel 1970, S. 133–135; Mary Snell, *Vom Lesen zum Interpretieren am Beispiel englischer Lyrik*, München 1972, S. 37–39.

THOMAS GRAY

26. 12. 1716 London – 30. 7. 1771 Cambridge

Thomas Gray war das fünfte und einzige überlebende Kind eines Notars. Seine glücklichsten Jahre verbrachte er in Eton, wo er 1725 Richard West und Horace Walpole, den Sohn des ersten (damals noch nicht so genannten) englischen Premierministers, zu Freunden gewann. 1734–39 studierte er in Cambridge und brach dann mit Walpole zur *Grand Tour* nach Frankreich und Italien auf. Doch die beiden schieden 1741 im Streit. Auf der Rückreise schrieb Gray im Kloster von Chartreuse sein erstes bedeutendes Gedicht, eine alkäische Ode in lateinischer Sprache. In England erneuerte er seine Freundschaft mit West, dessen plötzlicher Tod im Mai 1742 eine fruchtbare schöpferische Phase auslöste. In rascher Folge entstanden die »Ode on a Distant Prospect of Eton College« (in der sich Formtraditionen der Ode mit denen des topographischen Gedichts à la John Denham verbinden), die »Hymn to Adversity« (in der sich der Einfluss des horazischen *carmen saeculare* niederschlägt) und das überragende Sonett des 18. Jahrhunderts, »Sonnet on the Death of Mr Richard West«. Daneben begann er mit der Arbeit an seinem bedeutendsten Werk, der »Elegy Written in a Country Churchyard« (abgeschlossen 1750). Aus Oxford, wo er sich inzwischen niedergelassen hatte, reiste er gelegentlich nach London, um sich im British Museum mit der altnordischen und keltischen Literatur vertraut zu machen. 1745 söhnte er sich mit Walpole aus, 1747 lehnte er das ihm angebotene Amt des Hofdichters ab. Das Jahr 1747 markiert zugleich das Ende seines dichterischen Wirkens, doch trug ihm sein Ruf als Literat und Historiker 1768, als die Gesamtausgabe seiner Werke erschien, eine Professur für Geschichte und neuere Sprachen in Cambridge ein. Da es sich um eine reine Sinekure handelte, war der scheue Dichter der Verpflichtung enthoben, Vorlesungen abzuhalten.

Formal steht Gray noch in der Tradition des Klassizismus, doch kündigt sich in seinen elegischen Werken bereits die Romantik an. Ton und Thema des Sonetts auf den Tod von West sind in einem Gedicht des verstorbenen Freundes vorweggenommen, der sich seinerseits auf einen späten Brief von Alexander Pope stützt, in dem es heißt: »The morning after my Exit, the sun will rise as bright as ever, the flowers smell as sweet, the plants spring as green, the world will proceed in its old course, people will laugh as heartily, and marry as fast as they were us'd to do«.

Text: Thomas Gray, *The Complete English Poems,* hrsg. von James Reeves, London: Heinemann, 1973.

Sekundärliteratur: Donald C. Mell, »Form as Meaning in Augustan Elegy: A Reading of Thomas Gray's ›Sonnet on the Death of Richard West‹«, in: *Papers on Language and Literature* 4 (1968) S. 131–143; James Reeves (Hrsg.), *The Complete English Poems of Thomas Gray,* London 1973, S. 9–11.

THOMAS HARDY

2.6.1840 Upper Bockhampton (Dorset) – 11.1.1928 Max Gate bei Dorchester

Thomas Hardy war Sohn eines Baumeisters und schlug zunächst die Architektenlaufbahn ein. Nach Abschluss der Lehrzeit in Dorchester (1856–62) übte er seinen Beruf zunächst in London (1862–1867), dann in Dorset (1867–70) aus. Er begann seine literarische Laufbahn in London, fand aber mit seinen Gedichten keine Anerkennung und wandte sich dem Roman zu. Der Durchbruch gelang ihm mit *A Pair of Blue Eyes* (1873), so dass er die Architektur aufgeben und heiraten konnte (1874). Auch die folgenden Erzählwerke fanden ein begeistertes Publikum, bis der Roman *Jude the Obscure* (1895), der heute den Meisterwerken *The Mayor of Casterbridge* (1886) und *Tess of the D'Urbervilles* (1891) an die Seite gestellt wird, wegen der Behandlung sexueller und ehelicher Probleme auf so heftige Kritik stieß, dass Hardy sich gezwungen sah, zu seiner ersten Liebe, der Lyrik, zurückzukehren. 1912 starb seine Frau, 1914 heiratete er ein zweites Mal. Die letzten Jahrzehnte verbrachte er in Stinsford (Dorset) und hielt ein offenes Haus für junge Dichter, die seinen Rat suchten.

Hardy knüpft in seiner Lyrik an regionale Traditionen an und bemüht sich um einen der Umgangssprache angenäherten Stil. Gerade weil er technisch nicht zu den besten englischen Lyrikern gehört, haben zahlreiche junge Dichter des 20. Jahrhunderts ihn zum Vorbild gewählt (Dylan Thomas, Larkin). Auden schrieb: »Much as I loved him, even I could see that his diction was often clumsy and forced and that a lot of his poems were plain bad. This gave me hope where a flawless poet might have made me despair.«

Im Sonett »A Church Romance« (1906) erinnert Hardy an die Brautzeit der Eltern, als der Vater sonntags in der Kirche Violine zu spielen pflegte.

Text: Thomas Hardy, *The Complete Poems,* hrsg. von James Gibson, London: Macmillan, 1978.

Sekundärliteratur: James O. Bailey, *The Poetry of Thomas Hardy: A Handbook and Commentary,* Chapel Hill 1970, S. 232–234; Rosemary L. Eakins, »The Mellstock Quire and Tess in Hardy's Poetry«, in: Patricia Clements / Juliet Grindle (Hrsg.), *The Poetry of Thomas Hardy,* London 1980, S. 52–68.

SEAMUS HEANEY

* 13. 4. 1939 Mossbawn, Co. Derry (Nordirland)

Seamus Heaney verbrachte seine Kindheit auf der elterlichen Farm im heute zu Großbritannien gehörenden Teil Ulsters und studierte nach dem Schulbesuch englische Literatur an der Queen's University in Belfast (1957–61). Er arbeitete zunächst als Lehrer an verschiedenen schulischen Institutionen in Belfast, später – unterbrochen von einer Gastprofessur an der University of California, Berkeley (1970/71) – als Dozent an seiner alten Universität. 1962 heiratete er. Als Heaney 1972 im Zuge der erneut ausbrechenden Unruhen in Ulster von Ian Paisley als papistischer Propagandist denunziert wurde, siedelte er mit Rücksicht auf seine Familie in die Republik Irland über, zunächst nach Glanmore (Co. Wicklow), 1976 nach Dublin, wo er noch heute wohnt. Bis 1975 lebte er als freischaffender Autor, 1975–81 arbeitete er wieder an einem Lehrerseminar. Seit 1982 wirkt er als *poet in residence,* seit 1984 auch als Rhetorikprofessor an der Universität Harvard, 1989–94 war er Professor für Dichtkunst in Oxford. Seine Essays und Vorlesungen liegen gesammelt vor in den Bänden *Preoccupations* (1980), *The Government of the Tongue* (1988) und *The Place of Writing* (1989). 1995 erhielt er als erster irischer Lyriker seit Yeats den Nobelpreis.

In seinem berühmt gewordenen frühen Gedicht »Digging« (publ. 1966) stellt Heaney sich bewusst in die Tradition seiner bäuerlichen Vorfahren. Das Moor wird zur zentralen Metapher seines Werkes, er selbst zum Archäologen der Gewalt in Irland. In »Exposure« (publ. 1975) legt er dar, wie es ihm nicht einmal in der inneren Emigration gelingt, sich den politischen Verhältnissen zu entziehen. Von *exposure* ›Ausgesetztsein, Preisgabe‹ ist auch im hier vorgestellten Liebesgedicht aus den *Glanmore Sonnets* (1979) die Rede. Die landschaftliche Szenerie des Sonetts lässt an eine Bemerkung Heaneys denken, derzufolge seine Gedichte wie Moorleichen im Moor der Einbildungskraft emporsteigen. Martin Mosebach nennt ihn einen »Sänger des Gewesenen: des verflossenen Lebens- und Liebesmoments, der verlorenen Religion, der untergegangenen Bilder.«

Wichtigste Lyrikbände: *Death of a Naturalist* (1966); *Door into the Dark* (1969); *Wintering Out* (1972); *North* (1975); *Field Work* (1979); *Station Island* (1984); *The Haw Lantern* (1987); *Seeing Things* (1991); *The Spirit Level* (1996).

Text: Seamus Heaney, *Field Work*, London: Faber and Faber, 1979. Reprinted by permission of Faber and Faber Ltd., London.

Sekundärliteratur: Neil Corcoran, *Seamus Heaney*, London 1986, S. 142–149; Thomas C. Foster, *Seamus Heaney*, Boston 1989, S. 94–98; Michael Parker, *Seamus Heaney: The Making of a Poet*, London 1993, S. 166–172, 260 f.; Daniel Tobin, *Passage to the Center: Imagination and the Sacred in the Poetry of Seamus Heaney*, Lexington 1999, S. 155–162, 313.

GEORGE HERBERT

3. 4. 1593 Montgomery Castle (Wales) – 3. 3. 1633 Bemerton (Wiltshire)

George Herbert stammte aus einer adligen walisisch-normannischen Familie. Seine Mutter, Lady Magdalen Herbert, war – wie sein älterer Bruder Edward, Lord Herbert of Cherbury – mit Donne befreundet (Donnes Sonettzyklus *La Corona* ist Lady Herbert gewidmet). Nach dem frühen Tod des Vaters wurde er von der Mutter erzogen, besuchte die Westminster School und studierte am Trinity College in Cambridge (B.A. 1612, M.A. 1616), wo er 1618–20 als Dozent für Rhetorik und 1620–27 als *public orator* (d. h. als Redner bei feierlichen Anlässen) tätig war. Um 1627 wurde er zum Diakon geweiht und zog sich aus dem öffentlichen Leben zurück. 1630 erhielt er die Pfarrstelle von Bemerton (bei Salisbury) und empfing die Priesterweihe. Bei seiner Gemeinde als pflichtbewusster Seelenhirte äußerst beliebt, schrieb er in seinen freien Stunden geistliche Gedichte, die wenige Monate nach seinem Tod unter dem Titel *The Temple* publiziert wurden und starken Einfluss auf die Lyrik seiner jüngeren Zeitgenossen Richard Crashaw und Henry Vaughan ausübten.

Die von den Biographen gerühmte Demut des Dichters dürfte ebenso das Ergebnis geistlicher Disziplin wie natürlicher Veranlagung gewesen sein. Diesen Eindruck vermitteln jedenfalls Gedichte wie »Nature« und »The Collar«, in denen er die Auflehnung gegen Gott und Gottes Gebote zum Thema macht. Doch selbst diesen Gedichten fehlt der dramatische Ton seines Vorbildes Donne. Umgekehrt strahlt der manchmal das Hysterische streifende Donne nichts von Herberts kontemplativer Ruhe und

Gelassenheit aus. T. S. Eliot hat den Unterschied der beiden *metaphysicals* treffend benannt: »Both men were highly intellectual, both men had very keen sensibility: but in Donne thought seems in control of feeling, and in Herbert feeling seems in control of thought.«

Text: George Herbert, *The Works,* hrsg. von F. E. Hutchinson, Oxford: Clarendon Press, 1941.

Sekundärliteratur: Hans Combecher, *Deutung englischer Gedichte,* Bd. 2, Frankfurt a. M. 1965, S. 51–55; Arno Esch, *Englische religiöse Lyrik des 17. Jahrhunderts: Studien zu Donne, Herbert, Crashaw, Vaughan*, Tübingen 1955, S. 75 f.; Barbara L. Harman, *Costly Monuments: Representations of the Self in George Herbert's Poetry*, Cambridge (Mass.) 1982, S. 80–83, 206 f.; Virginia R. Mollenkott, »George Herbert's ›Redemption‹«, in: *English Language Notes* 10 (1973) S. 262–267; Helen Wilcox, »›All Things Are Big with Jest‹: Irony in Herbert's *Temple*«, in: H. W. / Richard Todd (Hrsg.), *George Herbert: Sacred and Prophane*, Amsterdam 1995, S. 127–140.

GERARD MANLEY HOPKINS

28. 7. 1844 Stratford (Essex) – 8. 6. 1889 Dublin

Gerard Manley Hopkins war das älteste von acht Kindern eines Versicherungskaufmanns, den er als Schüler zweimal nach Deutschland begleitete (1857, 1860). Am Balliol College in Oxford, wo Arnold und Pater zu seinen Lehrern gehörten, studierte er Altphilologie (1863–67), freundete sich mit Robert Bridges an und konvertierte unter dem Einfluss Newmans (1866). Nach seinem vorzüglichen Examen reiste er zunächst nach Paris (1867) und lehrte dann auf Einladung seines Mentors Newman am Priesterseminar in Birmingham (1867/68). 1868 entschloss er sich, selbst Priester zu werden, vernichtete sein dichterisches Frühwerk und wurde im September 1868 in den Jesuitenorden aufgenommen. Nach dem Studium der Philosophie in Stonyhurst (1870–73) arbeitete er als Rhetorik-Lehrer in Roehampton (1873/74) und studierte Theologie am St. Beuno's College (Nordwales). Als beim Untergang des Segelschiffs *Deutschland* in der Themsemündung im Dezember 1875 fünf Franziskanerinnen ums Leben kamen, äußerte sein Rektor den Wunsch, es möge jemand ein Gedicht über dieses Ereignis schreiben. Hopkins verstand dies als Aufforderung, sein dichterisches Schweigen zu brechen, und schrieb sein erstes Meisterwerk, »The Wreck of the Deutschland«. Im September 1877 wurde er zum Priester geweiht und arbeitete in den nächsten Jahren als Seelsorger und Prediger in Sheffield, Stonyhurst, London, Oxford, Bedford Leigh (bei Manchester) und in den Slums von Liverpool. 1881/82 zog er sich zu Exerzitien nach Roehampton zurück, 1882–1884 lehrte er alte Sprachen am Stonyhurst College und wurde 1884 Professor für Altphilologie am University College in Dublin. Im April 1889 erkrankte er an Typhus und starb zwei Monate später.

1918 hielt Robert Bridges den Zeitpunkt für gekommen, die Gedichte des Freundes mit einem apologetischen Vorwort zu publizieren, doch erst die zweite Auflage fand die gebührende Resonanz. Hopkins' Technik (Ellipsen, Sprungrhythmus, gespaltene Reime) hat die Lyrik des 20. Jahrhunderts von Auden über Barker und Dylan Thomas bis zu Ted Hughes stark beeinflusst. Einen wesentlichen Beitrag zum Verständnis der Dichtung leisten Hopkins' Briefe an Bridges und R.W. Dixon.

Text: Gerard Manley Hopkins, *Poems and Prose,* hrsg. von W. H. Gardner, Harmondsworth: Penguin, 1975 ([1]1953).

Sekundärliteratur: Peter Hühn, *Geschichte der englischen Lyrik,* Bd. 2, Tübingen 1995, S. 98–110 [zu »The Windhover«]; Wolfgang Iser, »Gerard Manley Hopkins: Zwischen Romantik und Moderne«, in: Rudolf Sühnel / Dieter Riesner (Hrsg.), *Englische Dichter der Moderne: Ihr Leben und Werk*, Berlin 1971, S. 33–51 [zu »The Windhover«]; Kunio Shimane, »The Sonnet of ›Endeavour‹: ›Thou art indeed just, Lord‹«, in: *Hopkins Quarterly* 7 (1980) S. 65–81; Graham Storey, *A Preface to Hopkins*, London 1981, S. 111 f. [zu »Felix Randal«]; Theodor Wolpers, »Gerard Manley Hopkins' ›The Windhover‹ zwischen Tradition und Moderne«, in: Karl Josef Höltgen, Lothar Hönnighausen [u. a.] (Hrsg.), *Tradition und Innovation in der englischen und amerikanischen Lyrik des 20. Jahrhunderts*, Tübingen 1986, S. 1–17.

JOHN KEATS

31.10.1795 London – 23.2.1821 Rom

John Keats war der älteste Sohn eines Mietstallbesitzers. Nach dem frühen Tod des Vaters heiratete die Mutter erneut und überließ die Erziehung der Kinder den Großeltern. Keats besuchte eine ausgezeichnete Internatsschule (1802–09) und begann danach eine medizinische Ausbildung am Londoner Guy's Hospital, die er 1816 abschloss. Trotz seiner Armut arbeitete er nicht als Arzt, sondern wandte sich der Lyrik zu. Seine letzten Lebensjahre waren überschattet vom Tod des jüngsten Bruders Tom, der unerfüllten Liebe zur jungen Fanny Brawne, vernichtenden Rezensionen seiner Dichtung und einem tödlichen Lungenleiden. Dennoch blieb seine schöpferische Kraft bis zu seiner Reise nach Italien im September 1820 ungebrochen. Er starb in Rom im Beisein seines Freundes Joseph Severn.

Die ersten überlieferten Verse schrieb Keats im Alter von achtzehn Jahren: Imitationen der Mittelalter-Nostalgie *The Faerie Queene* des bewunderten Spenser. Von Spenser, später auch von Shakespeare und Milton angeregt, schuf er eine poetische Welt, die bis heute nichts von ihrem sinnlichen Zauber verloren hat. Die Schlüsselbegriffe seiner in Briefen fragmentarisch vorliegenden Poetologie lauten: Intensität (*intensity*), Wahrheit (*truth*) und Schönheit (*beauty*). Das wesentlichste Merkmal des Dichters bezeichnet er als *negative capability,* die Fähigkeit, »in Unsicherheit, Mysterien und Zweifeln auszuharren, ohne nervöses Verlangen nach Tat- und Ursache«.

Keats' Hauptwerke sind die 1819 entstandenen Oden (»Ode to a Nightingale«, »Ode on a Grecian Urn«, »To Autumn«), das Erzählgedicht »The Eve of Saint Agnes« (1819), die beiden Hyperion-Fragmente *Hyperion: A Fragment* (1818/19) und *The Fall of Hyperion* (1819), die Ballade »La Belle Dame Sans Merci« (1819) und die hier vorgestellten Sonette.

Text: John Keats, *The Complete Poems* hrsg. von John Barnard, Harmondsworth: Penguin, [3]1988.

Sekundärliteratur: John Barnard, *John Keats*, Cambridge 1987, S. 127–129, 163 [zu »Bright star«]; Michael Hanke, »John Keats in Deutschland«, in: Christine Fischer / Ulrich Steltner (Hrsg.), *Die Rezeption europäischer und amerikanischer Lyrik in Deutschland*, Frankfurt a. M. 1997, S. 33–52 [zu »On First Looking«]; Peter

Hühn, *Geschichte der englischen Lyrik,* Bd. 1, Tübingen 1995, S. 372–376 [zu »On First Looking«]; Teut Andreas Riese, »John Keats, Benjamin Haydon und die Parthenonskulpturen: Freundschaftsadresse und Kunstanschauung in den ›Elgin-Marbles-Sonetten‹«, in: T. A. R. / Dieter Riesner (Hrsg.), *Versdichtung der englischen Romantik: Interpretationen*, Berlin 1968, S. 334–367 [zu »On Seeing«]; Rudolf Sühnel, »Keats's ›On First Looking into Chapman's Homer‹«, in: Michael Gassenmeier / Petra Bridzun [u. a.] (Hrsg.), *British Romantics as Readers*, Heidelberg 1998, S. 35–41; Helmut Viebrock, *John Keats*, Darmstadt 1977, S. 83–87 [zu »On First Looking«]; Lawrence J. Zillman, *John Keats and the Sonnet Tradition: A Critical and Comparative Study*, New York 1966 ([1]1939).

PHILIP LARKIN

9. 8. 1922 Coventry – 2. 12. 1985 Hull

Philip Larkin wurde als zweites Kind eines wohlhabenden Kommunalbeamten geboren und studierte am St. John's College in Oxford englische Literatur (1940–43). Seit 1943 arbeitete er als Bibliothekar, von 1955 bis zu seinem Tod an der Universitätsbibliothek in Hull. In der epigonalen ersten Lyriksammlung *The North Ship* (1945) bewegte er sich noch auf den Pfaden von Yeats. Es folgten zwei Romane, *Jill* (1946) und *A Girl in Winter* (1947), die zwar wohlwollend, aber wenig enthusiastisch rezensiert und kaum gelesen wurden. Schlagartig berühmt wurde er dagegen mit der Lyriksammlung *The Less Deceived* (1955). Hier waren die Forderungen der jungen Dichter der fünfziger Jahre (*movement poets*) nach umgangssprachlicher Diktion und rationaler Fasslichkeit in metrisch formvollendeten Versen eingelöst. Larkin hielt das eroberte Terrain mühelos, ohne je vom Ehrgeiz getrieben zu werden, es zu erweitern. Seinem bescheidenen Auftreten entsprechend, neigte er dazu, sein Talent selbstironisch herunterzuspielen: »Please don't think I'm great«, fiel er einmal einem Interviewer ins Wort. Doch ist er keineswegs der auf Hardy fixierte Provinzlyriker, auf den ihn bescheidener talentierte Kollegen wie Charles Tomlinson zu reduzieren versucht haben. Seine Dichtung der sechziger und siebziger Jahre beweist, dass er, eigenen Bekenntnissen zum Trotz, kontinentale Autoren (insbesondere die französischen Symbolisten) gern und mit unfehlbarem Instinkt für

Chancen und Gefahren ihres Einflusses gelesen hat. Öffentliche Anerkennung hat er mehrfach erfahren. So wurde er mit der Edition des *Oxford Book of Twentieth Century English Verse* (1973) betraut, 1976 erhielt er den Hamburger Shakespeare-Preis, 1984 wurde ihm nach dem Tod seines Freundes John Betjeman das Amt des Hofdichters angeboten, das er jedoch ausschlug.

»Larkins Qualitäten liegen in der Schärfe der Beobachtung, seiner Ironie, der konzisen und kadenzierten Sprache, der Dichte der Aussage, der formalen Virtuosität und der Treffsicherheit seiner Bilder« (Arno Esch). Er hat wesentlich dazu beigetragen, die oft beklagte Kluft zwischen dem modernen Dichter und seinem Publikum zu schließen. Wie ihm dies gelingt, zeigt das hier vorgestellte Gemäldesonett, eine Genreszene, in der die originelle Motivik mit einem in der neueren Lyrik nicht allzu oft anzutreffenden Sinn für Humor gehandhabt wird.

Wichtigste Lyrikbände: *The North Ship* (1945); *The Less Deceived* (1955); *The Whitsun Weddings* (1964); *High Windows* (1974). – (Postum) *Collected Poems,* hrsg. von Anthony Thwaite (1988).

Text: Philip Larkin, *High Windows*, London: Faber and Faber, 1974. Reprinted by permission of Faber and Faber Ltd., London.

Sekundärliteratur: Roger Day, *Larkin*, Milton Keynes 1987, S. 66–68; Salem K. Hassan, *Philip Larkin and his Contemporaries*, London 1988, S. 123–126, 196 f.; Rainer Lengeler, »Philip Larkin: ›The Card-Players‹«, in: R. L. (Hrsg.), *Englische Literatur der Gegenwart 1971–1975*, Düsseldorf 1977, S. 345–347.

ALICE MEYNELL

22. 9. 1847 Barnes (bei London) – 27. 11. 1922 London

Alice Meynell verbrachte den größten Teil ihrer Jugend in Italien und Frankreich, konvertierte und heiratete 1877 den Verleger, Zeitschriftenherausgeber und Lyriker Wilfrid Meynell, mit dem sie acht Kinder hatte. Ihre ersten kritisch-belletristischen Aufsätze erschienen in den Zeitschriften ihres Mannes, den ersten Lyrikband publizierte sie 1875 (*Preludes*). Die Meynells waren mit zahlreichen bedeutenden Schrifstellern ihrer Zeit befreundet (Browning, Rossetti, Ruskin, Tennyson) und gewährten jungen Dichtern großzügige materielle und seelische Unterstützung. Francis Thompson, Verfasser des berühmten Gedichts »The Hound of Heaven«, verdankt ihnen nach einer Phase der Armut und Drogensucht die Rückkehr in ein geregeltes Leben. Neben zahlreichen Essays schrieb Alice Meynell religiöse Lyrik, die in ihrer unprätentiösen Schlichtheit und Transparenz an Christina Rossetti erinnert.

Text: Alice Meynell, *The Poems*, London: Oxford University Press, 1940.

Sekundärliteratur: Terence L. Connolly (Hrsg.), *Alice Meynell Centenary Tribute, 1847–1947*, Boston 1948; Beverly Ann Schlack, »The ›Poetess of Poets‹: Alice Meynell Rediscovered«, in: *Women's Studies* 7 (1980) S. 111–126.

JOHN MILTON

9. 12. 1608 London – 8. 11. 1674 London

John Milton war Sohn eines wohlhabenden Notars und besuchte nach erstem Unterricht im Haus des Vaters die St. Paul's School. 1625–32 studierte er am Christ's College in Cambridge, wo das später von Händel vertonte Oden-Paar »L'Allegro« und »Il Penseroso« (1631?) entstand. 1632–38 betrieb er theologische und philosophische Studien, schrieb die Ode »At a Solemn Music« (1633?), das höfische Maskenspiel *Comus* (1634) und die Pastoralelegie »Lycidas« (1637). 1638/39 hielt er sich in Italien auf, von wo ihn der Ausbruch des Bürgerkriegs zurückrief. Er ließ sich in London nieder und heiratete (1642). In zahlreichen Pamphleten setzte er sich für diverse Freiheitsrechte ein. Besonders am Herzen lag ihm die Reformierung des Scheidungsrechts (*The Doctrine and Discipline of Divorce,* 1643), da er seiner Ehefrau überdrüssig war, wie überhaupt sein Verhältnis zu Frauen die Neugier der Biographen geweckt hat: Er bewunderte weibliche Schönheit und Intelligenz, wenn er sie außerhalb seines Hauses antraf, und misshandelte die eigenen Töchter. Als Puritaner und Parteigänger Cromwells griff er den anglikanischen Klerus an, unterbreitete Vorschläge für eine Bildungsreform (*Of Education,* 1644) und machte sich zum Sprecher für Pressefreiheit (*Areopagitica,* 1644). Als Außenminister des Commonwealth verteidigte er die Hinrichtung Karls I. (*Defence of the English People,* 1651) und Cromwells brutales Vorgehen gegen die irische Zivilbevölkerung. 1652 starb seine Frau, er selbst erblindete. 1656 schloss er eine zweite Ehe und begann mit der Arbeit an seinem Hauptwerk, dem Versepos *Paradise Lost.* 1658 starb auch die zweite Frau. Nach der Restauration 1660 wurde er kurz in den Tower eingewiesen. 1663 folgte die dritte Heirat, 1665 zwang ihn die Große Pest zur Flucht aus London, 1667 publizierte er *Paradise Lost,* 1671 *Paradise Regained* und *Samson Agonistes.* Aus Furcht, Karl II. könne ihn wegen der Hinrichtung seines Vaters zur Verantwortung ziehen, wagte er sich in den letzten Jahren kaum noch aus dem Haus. »As a man, he is antipathetic«, resümiert Eliot, hebt aber seine überragende Bedeutung als Dichter hervor. In Miltons Sonetten liegt der Akzent auf politischen und persönlichen Themen.

Text: John Milton, *The Poems,* hrsg. von John Carey und Alastair Fowler, London: Longmans, 1968.

Sekundärliteratur: E. J. A. Honigmann (Hrsg.), *Milton's Sonnets*, London 1966; Laurence Lerner, *An Introduction to English Poetry: Fifteen Poems Discussed*, London 1975, S. 77–86 [zu »When I consider«]; J. S. Smart, *The Sonnets of Milton*, Oxford 1966 ([1]1921); Leo Spitzer, »Understanding Milton« (1951), in: L. S., *Essays on English and American Literature,* hrsg. von Anna Hatcher, Princeton 1962, S. 116–131 [zu »Methought I saw«]; Hermann J. Weiand, »›On the late Massacre in Piedmont‹«, in: Reinhold Schiffer / H. J. W. (Hrsg.), *Insight III: Analyses of English and American Poetry,* Frankfurt a. M. 1969, S. 211–215; Egon Werlich, *Poetry Analysis: Great English Poems Interpreted*, Dortmund 1967, S. 41–62 [zu »When I consider«].

WILFRED OWEN

18. 3. 1893 Oswestry (Shropshire) – 4. 11. 1918 bei Ors (Frankreich)

Wilfred Owen stammte aus einer Familie der Mittelklasse (der Vater war zeitweilig Bahnhofsvorsteher in einem Vorort von Liverpool). Schon als Schüler vielseitig interessiert (Botanik, Astronomie, Geologie und Literatur), schrieb er seine ersten Gedichte unter dem Einfluss von Keats. Nach dem Studium in London und der Arbeit als kirchlicher Sozialhelfer war er 1913–15 Hauslehrer bei einer französischen Familie in Bordeaux. Im Oktober 1915 meldete er sich als Kriegsfreiwilliger und wurde 1917 als Frontoffizier in Frankreich eingesetzt. Nach einem schweren Angriff im April 1917 brach er mit einem Nervenschock zusammen und wurde im Juni ins Offiziershospital Craiglockhart überwiesen. Dort lernte er den Dichter Siegfried Sassoon kennen, der wegen seiner Kritik an der militärischen Führung nur knapp dem Erschießungskommando entronnen war. Für Owen war er »Keats + Christus + Elias + mein Oberst + mein Beichtvater + Amenophis IV im Profil«. Sassoon ermutigte ihn, seine Kriegserfahrungen dichterisch zu gestalten, und stand ihm dabei beratend zur Seite. Der Titel des Sonetts »Anthem for Doomed Youth« (1917) stammt von Sassoon, der sich später an die erste Lektüre erinnert: »I now realised that his verse, with its sumptuous epithets and large-scale imagery, its noble naturalness and the depth of meaning, had impressive affinities with Keats, whom he took as his supreme exemplar.« Im August 1918 kehrte Owen an die Front zurück, erhielt im Oktober das Military Cross für besondere Tapferkeit und fiel eine Woche vor dem Waffenstillstand bei der Überquerung eines Flusses in Flandern.

Owens Kriegslyrik zeichnet sich durch stilistische und prosodische Neuerungen (Halbreime, Konsonanzen) aus, die seiner an Keats geschulten Neigung zu metrischer Glätte entgegenwirken. Zu den besten späten Gedichten, »Flaschenpost aus dem Niemandsland zwischen Leben und Tod« (Rudolf Sühnel), gehören neben dem hier vorgestellten Sonett die im letzten Lebensjahr entstandenen *anthology pieces* »Strange Meeting«, »Futility«, »Greater Love« und »Disabled«. »Anthem for Doomed Youth« wurde neben anderen Owen-Gedichten von Benjamin Britten im *War Requiem* (1962) vertont.

Text: *The Complete Poems and Fragments of Wilfred Owen,* Bd. 1: *The Poems,* hrsg. von Jon Stallworthy, London: Chatto & Windus, The Hogarth Press / Oxford: Oxford University Press, 1983.

Sekundärliteratur: Claas Kazzer, »Wilfred Owen: ›Anthem for Doomed Youth‹«, in: Michael Hanke (Hrsg.), *Englische Gedichte des 20. Jahrhunderts: Interpretationen*, Stuttgart 1997, S. 125–131; Rudolf Sühnel, »Wilfred Owens ›Anthem for Doomed Youth‹«, in: Stefan Horlacher / Marion Islinger (Hrsg.), *Expedition nach der Wahrheit*, Heidelberg 1996, S. 243–248.

CHRISTINA ROSSETTI

5.12.1830 London – 29.12.1894 London

Christina Rossetti, die Schwester von Dante Gabriel Rossetti, war das jüngste von vier Kindern eines Kunst liebenden italienischen Freiheitskämpfers und Literaten, der am Londoner King's College als Professor für Italienisch wirkte. Ihre Erziehung verdankt sie der Mutter, deren Religiosität sie tief beeindruckte. Schon als Kind begann sie, Gedichte in englischer und italienischer Sprache zu schreiben. Nach dem Tod des Vaters (1854) half sie der Mutter als Lehrerin an einer Tagesschule und widmete sich kirchlichen und karitativen Aufgaben. 1862 publizierte sie ihren ersten Gedichtband *Goblin Market and Other Poems,* der autobiographische Züge aufweist. Ihre weiteren Sammlungen – darunter auch Kindergedichte – erschienen 1866, 1872, 1881 und 1893. Christina Rossettis Leben und Werk sind beherrscht von religiösen Konflikten. Sie bekannte sich zur hochkirchlichen Richtung der Church of England, die sich in Fragen des Ritus am Katholizismus orientiert. Aus Glaubensgründen lehnte sie zwei Heiratsanträge ab und führte ein zunehmend kontemplativ-asketisches Leben. Sie starb nach langer Krankheit.

Über ein halbes Jahrhundert stand sie im Schatten ihres Bruders Dante Gabriel. Doch 1961 schrieb James Reeves: »If there is ever a wholehearted revival of Victorian poetry, her genuine lyric gift and her delicate workmanship will once more receive their due.« Seither ist das Interesse an ihrem Werk auch in Deutschland stetig gewachsen, und ihr 14-teiliger Sonettzyklus *Monna Innominata* (1868?) wird als ein Hauptwerk religiöser Dichtung in England anerkannt. Auch außerhalb dieser Sequenz schrieb sie Lyrik, in der die geistig-seelische Spannung, in der sie lebte, überzeugenden Niederschlag gefunden hat. Dazu gehört »From Sunset to Star Rise« (1865). In wieder anderen Sonetten erzielt sie mit ironischen Wendungen Verfremdungseffekte, in der sich die Dichtung der Moderne anzukündigen scheint.

Text: Christina Rossetti, *The Complete Poems: A Variorum Edition,* 2 Bde., hrsg. von R. W. Crump, Baton Rouge: Louisiana State University Press, 1979, 1986.

Sekundärliteratur: Diane D'Amico, »Christina Rossetti's ›From Sunset to Star Rise‹: A New Reading«, in: *Victorian Poetry* 27 (1989) S. 95–100; Katherine J. Mayberry, *Christina Rossetti and the*

Poetry of Discovery, Baton Rouge 1989; Dolores Rosenblum, *Christina Rossetti: The Poetry of Endurance*, Carbondale 1986; Sharon Smulders, *Christina Rossetti Revisited*, New York 1996; William Whitla, »Questioning the Convention: Christina Rossetti's Sonnet Sequence *Monna Innominata*«, in: David A. Kent (Hrsg.), *The Achievement of Christina Rossetti*; Ithaca 1987, S. 82–131.

DANTE GABRIEL ROSSETTI

12. 5. 1828 London – 9. 4. 1882 Birchington-on-Sea (Kent)

Dante Gabriel Rossetti, der ältere Bruder Christina Rossettis, war Sohn eines Kunst liebenden italienischen Freiheitskämpfers und Literaten, der am Londoner King's College als Professor für Italienisch wirkte. 1841 begann er ein Kunststudium an der Royal Academy, wurde jedoch von deren Lehrmethoden abgestoßen und gründete 1848 mit einer Gruppe gleichaltriger Maler und Bildhauer die Bruderschaft der Präraffaeliten (*Pre-Raphaelite Brotherhood*), die ihre Ideale bei Giotto (1266–1337) und anderen Künstlern der italienischen Frührenaissance verwirklicht sah. John Ruskin hielt seine schützende Hand über die jungen Enthusiasten. Ende der fünfziger Jahre lernte Rossetti die Dichter William Morris und Swinburne kennen, 1860 heiratete er nach zehnjähriger Verlobung die Verkörperung des präraffaelitischen Schönheitsideals, Elizabeth Siddall, obwohl er sich inzwischen in Jane Burden, die spätere Frau von Morris, verliebt hatte. 1861 wurde er Teilhaber der von Morris finanzierten kunstgewerblichen Werkstätten. 1862 starb seine Frau. Von Schuldgefühlen überwältigt, senkte er seine Gedichte mit ihr ins Grab und zog mit dem Bruder William, mit Swinburne und George Meredith zusammen. Meredith verließ jedoch die Wohngemeinschaft, als Rossetti das Haus und die Umgebung in einen zoologischen Garten (mit Zebu, Känguru, Waschbär u. dgl.) verwandelte. Infolge falscher medizinischer Behandlung wurde Rossetti drogenabhängig und zunehmend unberechenbar. 1869 ließ er seine Gedichte ausgraben und publizierte sie z.T. in den *Collected Poems* (1870), die von Robert Buchanan scharf angegriffen wurden (»The Fleshly School of Poetry«). Rossetti verteidigte sich zwar mit der glänzenden Replik »The Stealthy School of Criticism« (1871), wurde aber unter dem Eindruck ablehnender Kritik manisch depressiv. 1882 publizierte er seine zweite Lyriksammlung *Ballads and Sonnets,* die auch den

Zyklus *The House of Life* (101 Sonette) enthält. Seine Doppelbegabung als Maler und Dichter zeigt sich v. a. in den Begleitsonetten zu seinen eigenen Gemälden.

Rossettis einstiger Ruhm ist in dem Maße verblasst, in dem der seiner Schwester Christina gewachsen ist. Heutige Leser sind eher bereit, sich von seiner ungewöhnlichen Biographie als von seiner Dichtung fesseln zu lassen. Und doch: »Ridiculous as Rossetti was in his occult experiments, his fantastic collection of animals, his burial of his poems, and other eccentricities, there was something in his temperament which compels respect« (Roy Campbell). Respekt verdienen vor allem eine Hand voll Anthologiegedichte, darunter am italienischen Typus geschulte Sonette wie »Dawn on the Night-journey« (1855) oder das *déjà-vu*-Gedicht »Sudden Light«, dessen »denkwürdige Musikalität« von Jorge Luis Borges gerühmt wurde.

Text: Dante Gabriel Rossetti, *The Works,* hrsg. von William Michael Rossetti, London: Ellis, 1911.

Sekundärliteratur: Günther Jarfe, »Der geschrumpfte Augenblick: Einige Bemerkungen zu Dante Gabriel Rossettis ›Dawn on the Night-journey‹«, in: *Literatur in Wissenschaft und Unterricht* 12 (1979) S. 49–54.

WILLIAM SHAKESPEARE

23. (?) 4. 1564 Stratford-upon-Avon – 23. 4. 1616 Stratford-upon-Avon

Shakespeare war das dritte von acht Kindern angesehener Eltern. Der aus der *gentry* stammende Vater übte den Beruf eines Weißgerbers und Handschuhmachers aus; die Familie der Mutter (die Ardens) lässt sich bis auf Wilhelm den Eroberer zurückverfolgen. Vermutlich besuchte Shakespeare die *grammar school* von Stratford und lernte dort die alten Sprachen – wenn auch vielleicht weniger enthusiastisch als sein späterer Freund Ben Jonson, der ihm zu Unrecht eine mangelhafte klassische Bildung vorwarf. 1582 heiratete er die acht Jahre ältere Anne Hathaway, 1583 wurde die Tochter Susanna geboren, 1585 folgten Zwillinge. Nach einer biographischen Lücke von sieben Jahren wird Shakespeare erst 1592 wieder greifbar, und zwar in London, wo er inzwischen als renommierter Dramatiker, Schauspieler und Teilhaber der Theatertruppe The Lord Chamberlain's Men lebt. Großes Ansehen verschafft ihm die Publikation zweier dem Earl of Southampton gewidmeter Versepen, *Venus and Adonis* (1593) und *The Rape of Lucrece* (1594). Gegen Ende des 16. Jahrhunderts ist der »sweet swan of Avon« (Jonson) der beliebteste und finanziell erfolgreichste englische Dramatiker, bewundert und beneidet von zahllosen Rivalen.

Seine Dichtungstheorie, Weltanschauung und politische Einstellung hat Shakespeare nirgends niedergelegt. Versuche, sie seinen Dramen und Gedichten zu extrahieren, bleiben unbefriedigend und haben spekulationsfreudige Kritiker zu Annahmen verleitet, die den unbefangenen Leser das Staunen lehren. Dazu gehört die noch immer gelegentlich geäußerte Meinung, Shakespeares Stücke stammten von einem anderen. Auch über sein lyrisches Hauptwerk, den aus 154 Teilen bestehenden, 1609 vermutlich ohne seine Billigung publizierten Sonettzyklus, ist nicht nur Geistreiches zu Papier gebracht worden. Ungeklärt bleibt die Frage nach der Reihenfolge der Gedichte (man neigt heute dazu, sie in der Anordnung von 1609 zu belassen), ungeklärt die Identität des jungen Adligen, dem die ersten 126 Sonette gelten, ungeklärt auch die Identität der *dark lady*. Einigkeit aber besteht darin, dass der Zyklus Höhepunkt und Abschluss der englischen Petrarca-Rezeption bildet.

Text: William Shakespeare, *The Sonnets and A Lover's Complaint,* hrsg. von John Kerrigan, Harmondsworth: Penguin, 1995.

Sekundärliteratur: J. B. Leishman, *Themes and Variations in Shakespeare's Sonnets*, London 1961; Horst Meller, *Zum Verstehen englischer Gedichte*, München 1985, S. 35–55 [zum Sonett 130]; Ewald Standop, »Shakespeares Sonett 73: Analyse einer Analyse anstelle einer Rezension«, in: *Literatur in Wissenschaft und Unterricht* 19 (1986) S. 227–238; ders., »Shakespeares Sonett 65 in linguistischer Sicht«, in: Manfred Beyer (Hrsg.), *Zum Begriff der Imagination in Dichtung und Dichtungstheorie*, Trier 1998, S. 48–65, Theodor Wolpers, »William Shakespeare: Die Sonette«, in: Karl Heinz Göller (Hrsg.), *Die englische Lyrik: Von der Renaissance bis zur Gegenwart,* Bd. 1, Düsseldorf 1968, S. 76–133, 398–404 [zu den Sonetten 18, 29, 73, 116, 129, 146].

PERCY BYSSHE SHELLEY

4. 8. 1792 Field Place (Sussex) – 8. 7. 1822 Golf von La Spezia

Percy Bysshe Shelley entstammte einer wohlhabenden Aristokratenfamilie und genoss eine standesgemäße Erziehung in Eton (1804–10), wo der sensible und gesundheitlich anfällige Junge wegen seiner exzentrischen Lebensführung den Beinamen »mad Shelley« erhielt. Schon damals wandte er sich gegen jegliche Autorität in Kirche und Staat. 1810 begann er sein Studium am University College in Oxford, wo er unter dem Einfluss von William Godwins radikal-atheistischen Schriften sein Pamphlet *The Necessity of Atheism* (1811) schrieb. Shelley wurde sofort relegiert und heiratete im selben Jahr die sechzehnjährige Harriet Westbrook, mit der er ruhelos umherzog (Wales, Irland, London). 1814 entführte er Godwins Tochter Mary Wollstonecraft (Verfasserin von *Frankenstein,* 1818) in die Schweiz und heiratete sie nach Harriets Selbstmord (1816). Er begegnete Byron und bereiste mit ihm Italien (1818), wo er sich in Platos Philosophie vertiefte. Angeregt durch das »Peterloo Massacre« entstand 1819 die politische Allegorie »The Masque of Anarchy« (publ. 1832), im gleichen Jahr eine geistreich-humorvolle Satire auf Wordsworth (»Peter Bell the Third«). 1819 folgten zwei Versdramen (*The Cenci, Prometheus Unbound*) und die berühmte »Ode to the West Wind«. 1820 zog er nach Pisa, wo zahlreiche kürzere Gedichte entstanden, darunter »The Cloud« und »To a Skylark«, im April 1821 die Elegie »Adonais« auf den Tod von Keats. Ebenfalls 1821 publizierte er die im Titel auf Sidney zurückweisende Schrift *The Defence of Poetry,* in der er seine Gedanken vom Dichter als sozialem Reformator vortrug. Der berühmt gewordene Satz von den Dichtern als »inoffiziellen Gesetzgebern der Welt« (»unacklowledged legislators of the world«) knüpft an die antike Vorstellung vom gottähnlichen Status des Künstlers an. Anfang März 1822 zog Shelley mit seiner Familie nach Lerici und kam ein halbes Jahr später bei einem Segelunfall im Golf von La Spezia ums Leben.

Schon Wordsworth hat Shelleys Größe anerkannt (»one of the best *artists* of us all«), andere haben ihm fehlende menschliche und künstlerische Reife vorgeworfen. Wie dem auch sei: Zumindest Eliots Kritik, Metaphorik und Begrifflichkeit seiner Dichtung seien verwaschen, ist inzwischen widerlegt worden, am überzeugendsten in der Monographie des Naturwissenschaftlers Desmond King-Hele.

Text: Percy Bysshe Shelley, *The Complete Poetical Works,* hrsg. von Thomas Hutchinson, London: Oxford University Press, 1960 ([1]1905).

Sekundärliteratur: Michael Ferber, *The Poetry of Shelley,* Harmondsworth 1993, S. 108–111; Desmond King-Hele, *Shelley: The Man and the Poet,* New York 1960, S. 92–94; Rainer Lengeler, »Shelleys Sonett ›Ozymandias‹«, in: *Die Neueren Sprachen* N. F. 18 (1969) S. 532–539.

SIR PHILIP SIDNEY

30. 11. 1554 Penshurst (Kent) – 17. 10. 1586 Arnheim

Der aus adliger Familie stammende Sir Philip Sidney war als Höfling, Soldat, Gelehrter und Dichter schon zu Lebzeiten Inbegriff des idealen Renaissancemenschen, dem die Verbindung von *vita activa* und *vita contemplativa* mit scheinbar bewundernswerter Leichtigkeit gelang. Nach dem Schulbesuch, wo er mit seinem späteren Biographen Fulke Greville lebenslange Freundschaft schloss, trieb er natur- und geisteswissenschaftliche Studien am Christ Church College in Oxford, die er jedoch trotz glänzender Erfolge abbrach. Mit Billigung der Königin trat er eine Bildungsreise aufs Festland an, wo der charmante Aristokrat in Fürsten- und Königshäusern ein gern gesehener Gast war. Er war beim Vertragsschluss von Blois anwesend und erlebte als überzeugter Protestant die Bartholomäusnacht. Seine Reisen führten ihn weiter durch Deutschland, Österreich und Italien (1572–75) und zurück an den Hof der Königin. In ihrem Dienst hielt er sich in den folgenden Jahren noch mehrfach auf dem Kontinent auf und fiel in einem militärisch belanglosen Scharmützel gegen die Spanier in den Niederlanden.

Mit seinen Freunden Greville und Spenser fasste Sidney den ehrgeizigen Plan einer Erneuerung der Dichtkunst mit dem Ziel, auf englischem Boden eine der antiken gleichwertige Nationalliteratur zu stiften. Von der Undurchführbarkeit des Projekts legt der grandiose Torso von Spensers *Faerie Queene* Zeugnis ab. Sidneys Leistung mag bescheidener sein als die des Freundes, doch mit Blick auf seinen frühen Tod ist sie erstaunlich genug. Sein erstes größeres Werk war die epische Dichtung *Arcadia* (um 1580 entstanden, publiziert 1590, 1593), die sich das ganze 17. Jahrhundert hindurch großer Beliebtheit erfreute. Mit *Astrophel and Stella* (1581/82, publiziert 1591) schrieb er den ersten geschlossenen Sonettzyklus in englischer Sprache, der die Sonettlawine der folgenden Jahre (darunter die Zyklen von Daniel und Drayton) auslöste. Die Frage, inwieweit seine Freundschaft zu Lady Rich die Entstehung seiner Sonette beeinflusst hat, ist irrelevant, seitdem die Forschung nachgewiesen hat, dass »der Wille zur kunstvollen Behandlung traditioneller Themen die lyrische Selbstaussage zurücktreten läßt« (Reimer Jehmlich). Mit seiner Poetik *An Apology for Poetry* (1595, rev. als *The Defence of Poesy*) legt er eine ethische Rechtfertigung des dichterischen Schaffens vor und erweist sich als bester englischer Literaturkritiker vor Dryden.

Text: Sir Philip Sidney, *The Poems,* hrsg. von William A. Ringler, Jr., Oxford: Clarendon Press, 1962.

Sekundärliteratur: Reimer Jehmlich, *Die Bildlichkeit in der Liebeslyrik Sir Philip Sidneys, Michael Draytons und John Donnes (»Astrophel and Stella«, »Idea«, »Songs and Sonets«)*, Diss. Kiel 1970, S. 153–155 [zu AS 31]; David Kalstone, *Sidney's Poetry: Contexts and Interpretations*, Cambridge (Mass.) 1965, S. 133–181; Horst Meller, *Zum Verstehen englischer Gedichte*, München 1985, S. 56–74 [zu AS 1]; Mary Snell, *Vom Lesen zum Interpretieren am Beispiel englischer Lyrik*, München 1972, S. 36 f. [zu AS 31].

EDMUND SPENSER

um 1552 London – 16. 1. 1599 London

Edmund Spenser war Sohn eines Londoner Schneiders. Nach dem Besuch der Merchant Taylors' School studierte er am Pembroke College in Cambridge alte und neue Sprachen und Literaturen (Italienisch, Französisch), Philosophie (Platon, Aristoteles, den italienischen Neuplatonismus) und Theologie. Unter den dort herrschenden Reformatoren wurde er zum Puritaner. Nach Abschluss der Studien stand er im Dienst des Earl of Leicester, freundete sich mit dessen Neffen Sir Philip Sidney an und erhielt 1580 eine Stelle als Privatsekretär bei Arthur Lord Grey, dem Statthalter der Königin in Irland, der die vermeintlichen irischen Rebellen grausam bekämpfte. Für seine militärischen Dienste und seine propagandistische Verteidigung der englischen Unterdrückungspolitik in Irland wird er mit einem Landgut in Kilcolman in der

Grafschaft Cork belohnt, das er jedoch 1598 bei einem weiteren Aufstand der Iren verliert. Erschöpft flüchtet er mit seiner Frau nach London, wo er ein Jahr später stirbt und in der Westminster Abbey beigesetzt wird.

Als Dichter tritt Spenser zunächst mit der epigonalen Eklogensammlung *The Shepheardes Calendar* (1579) hervor. Seine Heirat im Jahre 1594 führt zur Entstehung des Werbungszyklus *Amoretti* (89 Sonette) und seines besten Gedichts, des »Epithalamion« (beide 1595 publiziert). Ein weiteres Brautgedicht, das »Prothalamion«, entsteht 1596. Sein Hauptwerk aber ist das unvollendete, unter dem Einfluss von Tasso und Ariost geschriebene allegorische Versepos *The Faerie Queene* (um 1575–96), das er als Huldigung an die Königin und als Tugendlehre für die junge Aristokratie verstanden wissen wollte. Er schuf sich dafür sogar eine eigene Versform (die sog. Spenser-Stanze) und eine eigene Sprache, »die, indem sie reichlich archaische Wörter und manchmal auch Pseudo-Archaismen in sich aufnahm, weit vom alltäglich gesprochenen Idiom abrückte und den Leser, noch ehe er vernimmt, was eigentlich gesagt wird, in die geheimnisvoll-magische Ferne des Feenlandes versetzt« (Johannes Kleinstück). Dagegen stand die konzentrierte Form des Sonetts seiner Neigung zu epischer Breite und reichem sprachlichem Schmuck eher im Wege. Doch verdient sein Brautwerbungszyklus zumindest literarhistorisches Interesse, da es sich hier um eine domestizierte Variante der petrarkistischen Sonettdichtung handelt, in der die Konventionen der höfischen Liebe (Unerfüllbarkeit der Liebe, Gefühlskälte der Dame) – selbst wenn sie als motivische Elemente auftauchen – außer Kurs gesetzt werden.

Text: Edmund Spenser, *The Shorter Poems,* hrsg. von Richard A. McCabe, Harmondsworth: Penguin, 1999.

Sekundärliteratur: G. K. Hunter, »Spenser's *Amoretti* and the English Sonnet Tradition«, in: Judith M. Kennedy / James A. Reither (Hrsg.), *A Theatre for Spenserians*, Toronto 1973, S. 124–144; Ludwig W. Kahn, *Literatur und Glaubenskrise*, Stuttgart 1964, S. 68–70; Frank Erik Pointner, »Zur Entwicklung des englischen Sonetts in der Tudorzeit: Von der *imitatio* zur *emulatio* des italienischen Modells«, in: Theo Stemmler / Stefan Horlacher (Hrsg.), *Erscheinungsformen des Sonetts*, Tübingen 1999, S. 107–153, bes. S. 112–114.

HENRY HOWARD, EARL OF SURREY

1517 Kenninghall (?) (Norfolk) – 21. 1. 1547 London

Henry Howard entstammte einer angesehenen Adelsfamilie und wurde nach der Ernennung des Vaters zum Herzog von Norfolk als dessen ältester Sohn Graf Surrey. Vom väterlichen Privatsekretär erzogen, kam er an den Hof Heinrichs VIII., wurde von ihm mit dem Amt des Mundschenks betraut und heiratete 1532 die Tochter des Grafen Oxford. Der temperamentvolle Surrey war des Öfteren in Hofintrigen verwickelt und verbrachte die Jahre 1537–39 im Kerker von Windsor, wo ein großer Teil seiner Lyrik entstand. 1540 wurde er Turniermeister. Auf den Tod seines älteren Freundes Wyatt verfasste er die Klage »An Excellent Epitaph of Sir Thomas Wyatt« (1542). 1542–46 nahm er an Feldzügen in Schottland, Frankreich und Flandern teil, wurde in den Hosenbandorden aufgenommen, 1544 zum amtierenden Feldmarschall und 1545/46 zum Befehlshaber von Boulogne ernannt. Nach einer von ihm verschuldeten militärischen Niederlage kam es erneut zu Differenzen mit Heinrich, der ihn wegen Hochverrats vor Gericht stellen und verurteilen ließ. Nur acht Tage vor dem Tod seines despotischen Herrschers wurde Surrey auf dem Towerhügel hingerichtet. Die Gedichte wurden nach seinem Tod (mit denen seines Freundes Wyatt u. a.) in der Anthologie *The Book of Songs and Sonnets* (*Tottel's Miscellany*, 1557) publiziert.

Die englische Dichtung verdankt ihm die englisch reformierte Variante des Sonetts mit der Gliederung in drei Quartette und abschließendes Distichon sowie die Einführung des Blankverses in seinen Übersetzungen aus Vergils *Aeneis* (1540). Surreys Naturgedicht »The soote season, that bud and bloom forth brings« variiert, wie die meisten seiner Sonette, ein petrarkisches Vorbild. Die Motivik erinnert an den Prologbeginn von Chaucers *Canterbury Tales,* das Thema weist voraus auf das künstlerisch bedeutendere 115. Gedicht aus Tennysons *In Memoriam.*

Text: Henry Howard, Earl of Surrey, *Poems,* hrsg. von Emrys Jones, Oxford: Clarendon Press, 1964.

Sekundärliteratur: J. W. Lever, *The Elizabethan Love Sonnet*, New York [2]1974 ([1]1956), S. 42–45; Frank Erik Pointner, »Zur Entwicklung des englischen Sonetts in der Tudorzeit: Von der *imitatio* zur *emulatio* des italienischen Modells«, in: Theo Stemmler / Stefan Horlacher (Hrsg.), *Erscheinungsformen des Sonetts*, Tübingen

1999, S. 107–153, bes. S. 138–142; Hanspeter Schelp, »Henry Howard, Earl of Surrey: ›The soote season, that bud and blome furth bringes‹«, in: Karl Heinz Göller (Hrsg.), *Die englische Lyrik: Von der Renaissance bis zur Gegenwart*, Bd. 1, Düsseldorf 1968, S. 48–54, 395.

WILLIAM WORDSWORTH

7. 4. 1770 Cockermouth – 23. 4. 1850 Rydal Mount bei Grasmere

William Wordsworth war Sohn eines Gutsverwalters im Lake District und wuchs nach dem Tod der Mutter mit seinen Brüdern bei einer Quäkerin in Hawskhead auf. 1787 begann er sein Studium am St. John's College in Cambridge und schloss es nach einer Wanderung durch Frankreich, Schweiz und Italien 1791 mit einem mittelmäßigen Examen ab. Noch im selben Jahr kehrte er nach Frankreich zurück, wo er sich in Annette Vallon verliebte, die ihm eine Tochter (Caroline) schenkte. Er kehrte nach England zurück und blieb trotz der Septembermorde vorerst Anhänger der Französischen Revolution. Erst der Englisch-Französische Krieg und die dadurch erzwungene Trennung von Annette und Tochter Caroline weckten Schuldgefühle, die durch die enge Beziehung zu seiner Schwester Dorothy, die Freundschaft mit Coleridge (seit 1795) und eine Erbschaft etwas gemildert wurden. 1793 erschienen seine ersten Gedichte. 1795–98 lebte er mit seiner Schwester in Somerset und arbeitete mit Coleridge an den *Lyrical Ballads* (1798), die mit Wordsworths »Lines Written a Few Miles above Tintern Abbey« beschlossen werden. Die Publikation der 2. Auflage (1800) gilt als Geburtsstunde der englischen Romantik. Im Vorwort findet sich Wordsworths Deutung von der Lyrik als »spontanem Überfluss mächtiger Gefühle« (»spontaneous overflow of powerful feelings«) und vom Dichter als dem Sprecher aller Menschen. Den Winter 1798/99 verbrachte er mit Coleridge und Dorothy in Deutschland, wo er die »Lucy Poems« schrieb und mit der Arbeit an seinem autobiographischen Gedicht *The Prelude* (publ. postum 1850) über das »Reifen eines Dichtergeistes« begann. 1799 ließ er sich mit seiner Schwester in Grasmere im Lake District nieder, heiratete 1802 seine Schwägerin Mary Hutchinson, mit der er fünf Kinder hatte, und schrieb so bedeutende Gedichte wie »Resolution and Independence« (1802), die ersten beiden der hier vorgestellten Sonette, die »Ode: Intimations of Immortality« (1802–04), »I wandered lonely as a cloud« (1804, ohne die 2. Strophe), »The Solitary Reaper« (1804?) und die »Elegiac Stanzas« (1805), die alle in den *Poems in Two Volumes* (1807) publiziert wurden. Unter seiner späteren Lyrik findet vor allem das epische Gedicht *The Excursion* (publ. 1814) Anerkennung. 1843 wurde Wordsworth, fast schon Denkmal seiner selbst, als Nachfolger von Southey zum *poeta laureatus* ernannt.

Text: William Wordsworth, *The Poetical Works,* Bd. 3, hrsg. von E. de Selincourt und Helen Darbishire, Oxford: Clarendon Press, 1946.

Sekundärliteratur: Hans Combecher, *Deutung englischer Gedichte*, Bd. 2, Frankfurt a. M. 1965, S. 114–117 [zu »London, 1802«]; Lee M. Johnson, *Wordsworth and the Sonnet*, Kopenhagen 1973; Kurt Schlüter, »Wieder einmal ›Upon Westminster Bridge‹«, in: *Literatur in Wissenschaft und Unterricht* 12 (1979) S. 202–205; Egon Werlich, *Poetry Analysis: Great English Poems Interpreted*, Dortmund 1967, S. 85–100 [zu »Composed upon Westminster Bridge«]; Carl Woodring, *Wordsworth*, Cambridge (Mass.) 1968, S. 171 f. [zu »Surprised by joy«].

SIR THOMAS WYATT

1503 Allington Castle bei Maidstone (Kent) –
11. 10. 1542 Sherborne (Dorset)

Sir Thomas Wyatt entstammte einer adligen Familie und studierte um 1518 am St. John's College in Cambridge, bevor er sich an den Hof Heinrichs VIII. begab. Diplomatische Missionen im Auftrag des Königs führten ihn nach Frankreich, Italien und Spanien. 1528–32 war er Oberbefehlshaber von Calais, einem der wichtigsten englischen Stützpunkte auf dem Festland. 1537 empfing er den Ritterschlag. Kurz nach der Ernennung zum Vizeadmiral auf See starb er 1542 an einer fiebrigen Erkrankung.

Den königlichen Gunstbeweisen pflegten bei Wyatt die Erniedrigungen auf dem Fuße zu folgen. Wie viele andere Höflinge fiel auch er bei seinem launischen Herrscher des Öfteren in Ungnade und entging nur knapp dem Tode. Zweimal (1536 und 1541) war er im Tower eingekerkert. Im ersten Fall war er an seinem Schicksal möglicherweise nicht ganz unschuldig, falls der Verdacht zutreffen sollte, dass er ein Verhältnis mit Anne Boleyn, der zweiten

Frau des Königs und Mutter der späteren Elisabeth I., unterhalten hatte. Manche Biographen hegen den freilich unbeweisbaren Verdacht, sein Sonett »Who so list to hunt« könne unter dem Deckmantel einer Petrarca-Imitation auf eine solche Beziehung anspielen.

Wyatt gilt zwar als Vater des englischen Sonetts, doch schrieb er seine besten Gedichte, wenn er dem Formzwang der italienischen Vorbilder enthoben war. Er war ein begeisterter Experimentator, der sich in über siebzig, größtenteils selbst erfundenen Strophenformen übte, und zugleich der erste englische Lyriker, dem es gelang, eine unkonventionelle, auf persönlicher Erfahrung gründende Liebesdichtung zu schreiben. »A hand that taught what might be said in rhyme«, schrieb sein Freund Surrey, und zahlreiche spätere Lyriker haben sich ähnlich geäußert. Stephen Spender bezeichnete Wyatts berühmtestes Gedicht »They flee from me« als sein unerreichbares Vorbild, und Seamus Heaney spielt in seinem im vorliegenden Band abgedruckten Sonett darauf an.

Text nach: Sir Thomas Wyatt, *The Complete Poems,* hrsg. von R. A. Rebholz, Harmondsworth: Penguin, 1978.

Sekundärliteratur: Helmut Bonheim, »Notes on a Sonnet by Sir Thomas Wyatt«, in: *Literatur in Wissenschaft und Unterricht* 5 (1972) S. 1–5; Arthur F. Kinney, *Sir Thomas Wyatt*, Boston 1990, S. 97–100, 120; Frank Erik Pointner, »Zur Entwicklung des englischen Sonetts in der Tudorzeit: Von der *imitatio* zur *emulatio* des italienischen Modells«, in: Theo Stemmler / Stefan Horlacher (Hrsg.), *Erscheinungsformen des Sonetts*, Tübingen 1999, S. 107–153, bes. S. 108–112; Wolfgang Weiß, *Die elisabethanische Lyrik*, Darmstadt 1976, S. 74–76.

W. B. YEATS

13. 6. 1865 Dublin – 28. 1. 1939 Cap-Martin (Südfrankreich)

William Butler Yeats wuchs als Sohn eines anglo-irischen Malers in London auf, studierte Kunst in Dublin und schlug in den achtziger Jahren die Dichterlaufbahn ein. Sein Ziel war zunächst die Erneuerung der irischen Kultur auf der Grundlage der keltischen Mythologie. In den neunziger Jahren gehörte er zum Freundeskreis von Wilde, Dowson und Johnson, 1899 gründete er mit Lady Gregory in Dublin das irische Nationaltheater (das spätere Abbey

Theatre), an dem er seine Stücke aufführen ließ. Zudem wurde er als Förderer von Synge und O'Casey zu einem Führer der irischen Theaterbewegung. In diese Jahre fiel sein Bemühen um einen neuen lyrischen Stil. Er sagte sich los von den mythologischen Träumereien des Frühwerks und strebte nach einem härteren, am Gesprächsidiom gebildeten Stil, nach einer »kalten Schönheit«. Dabei erwies sich der junge Amerikaner Ezra Pound, der zeitweilig als sein Sekretär fungierte, als unermüdlicher Anreger und Ratgeber. Doch erst in den späten zwanziger Jahren gelangte Yeats zu der Überzeugung, mit dem Band *The Tower* (1928) sein Stilideal erreicht zu haben. Die Nachwelt hat diese Einschätzung übernommen.

Yeats wurde mehrfach geehrt – 1922 durch die Ernennung zum Senator des neuen irischen Freistaats, 1923 durch die Verleihung des Literaturnobelpreises. Er gilt heute neben Eliot als der bedeutendste englischsprachige Dichter des 20. Jahrhunderts. Privat erfuhr er manche Enttäuschung, darunter die zweimalige Ablehnung seines Heiratsangebots an die Schauspielerin Maud Gonne, deren Kampf für Irlands politische Unabhängigkeit er scharf ablehnte. Als eine Helena rediviva war sie inspirierendes Moment für einige seiner besten Gedichte, darunter das Sonett »Leda and the Swan« (1923), das sein lebenslanges Interesse an mythischen Stoffen und Motiven dokumentiert.

Wichtigste Lyrikbände: *The Wild Swans at Coole* (1919); *Michael Robartes and the Dancer* (1921); *The Tower* (1928); *Collected Poems* (1933); *The Winding Stair and Other Poems* (1933); *A Full Moon in March* (1935). – (Postum) *Last Poems* (1939); *Collected Poems* (2., erw. Aufl. 1950).

Text: W. B. Yeats, *The Collected Poems*, London: Macmillan, [2]1950.

Sekundärliteratur: Giorgio Melchiori, *The Whole Mystery of Art: Pattern into Poetry in the Work of W. B. Yeats*, London 1960, S. 73–163; Leo Spitzer, »On Yeats's Poem ›Leda and the Swan‹« (1954), in: L. S., *Essays on English and American Literature*, hrsg. von Anna Hatcher, Princeton 1962, S. 3–13; Rudolf Sühnel, »W. B. Yeats: ›Leda and the Swan‹«, in: Michael Hanke (Hrsg.), *Englische Gedichte des 20. Jahrhunderts: Interpretationen*, Stuttgart 1997, S. 46–53.

Literaturhinweise

I. *Anthologien*

Bender, Robert M. / Squier, Charles L. (Hrsg.), *The Sonnet: A Comprehensive Anthology of British and American Sonnets from the Renaissance to the Present*, New York 1965.

Evans, Maurice (Hrsg.), *Elizabethan Sonnets*, London 1977.

Feldman, Paula R. / Robinson, Daniel (Hrsg.), *A Century of Sonnets: The Romantic-Era Revival, 1750–1850*, New York 1999.

Fuller, John (Hrsg.), *The Oxford Book of Sonnets*, London 2000.

Grabes, Herbert (Hrsg.), *Elizabethan Sonnet Sequences*, Tübingen 1970. [Sidney, Daniel, Drayton, Spenser.]

Kallich, Martin / Ray, Jack C. / Rodney, Robert M. (Hrsg.), *A Book of the Sonnet: Poems and Criticism*, New York 1973.

Lever, J. W. (Hrsg.), *Sonnets of the English Renaissance*, London 1974.

Nye, Robert (Hrsg.), *The Faber Book of Sonnets*, London 1976.

White, Gertrude M. / Rosen, Joan G. (Hrsg.), *A Moment's Monument: The Development of the Sonnet*, New York 1972.

II. *Bibliographie*

Donow, Herbert S., *The Sonnet in England and America: A Bibliography of Criticism*, Westport (Conn.) 1982. [Nicht zum Sonett des 20. Jahrhunderts.]

III. *Sekundärliteratur*

Bullock, Walter L., »The Genesis of the English Sonnet Form«, in: *Publications of the Modern Language Association* 38 (1923) S. 729–744. [Zu Wyatt.]

Ferry, Anne, *The »Inward Language«: Sonnets of Wyatt, Sidney, Shakespeare, Donne*, Chicago 1983.

Fowler, Alastair, »Sonnet Sequences«, in: A. F., *Triumphal Forms: Structural Patterns in Elizabethan Poetry*, Cambridge 1970, S. 174–197. [Zu Sidney, Spenser, Shakespeare.]

Fuller, John, *The Sonnet*, London 1972. [Kurze Einführung.]

Furniss, Tom / Bath, Michael, »The Sonnet«, in: T. F. / M. B., *Reading Poetry: An Introduction*, London 1996, S. 280–304.

Fussell, Paul, »Structural Principles: The Example of the Sonnet«, in: P. F., *Poetic Metre and Poetic Form*, New York [2]1979 ([1]1965), S. 113–133.

Gassenmeier, Michael, »›Sonnetizing Dissonance‹: Die Zersingung der Erotik in englischsprachigen Sonetten des späten 19. und des frühen 20. Jahrhunderts«, in: Theo Stemmler / Stefan Horlacher (Hrsg.), *Erscheinungsformen des Sonetts*, Tübingen 1999, S. 155–179.

Going, William T., *Scanty Plot of Ground: Studies in the Victorian Sonnet*, Den Haag 1976.

Havens, Raymond D., »Milton and the Sonnet, with a History of the Sonnet in the Eighteenth and Early Nineteenth Centuries«, in: R. D. H., *The Influence of Milton on English Poetry*, New York 1961 ([1]1922), S. 478–548.

John, Lisle C., *The Elizabethan Sonnet Sequences: Studies in Conventional Conceits*, New York 1964 ([1]1938).

Lathrop, H. B., »The Sonnet Forms of Wyatt and Surrey«, in: *The Yale Review* 68 (1979) S. 383–393.

Lever, J. W., *The Elizabethan Love Sonnet*, London [2]1974 ([1]1956). [Zu Wyatt, Surrey, Sidney, Spenser, Shakespeare.]

Matthews, G. M., »Sex and the Sonnet«, in: *Essays in Criticism* 2 (1952) S. 119–137. [Antwort von Paul N. Siegel S. 465–468.]

Mönch, Walter, *Das Sonett: Gestalt und Geschichte*, Heidelberg 1955. [Standardwerk; zum englischen Sonett unbefriedigend.]

Neely, Carol Thomas, »The Structure of English Renaissance Sonnet Sequences«, in: *Journal of English Literary History* 45 (1978) S. 359–389.

Oppenheimer, Paul, *The Birth of the Modern Mind: Self, Consciousness, and the Invention of the Sonnet*, New York 1989.

Prince, F. T., »The Sonnet from Wyatt to Shakespeare«, in: John Russell Brown / Bernard Harris (Hrsg.), *Elizabethan Poetry*, London 1960, S. 11–29. (*Stratford-upon-Avon Studies*, 2.)

Richmond, W. K., *The English Sonnet*, London 1967.

Roche, Thomas P., *Petrarch and the English Sonnet Sequences*, New York 1989.

Siegel, Paul N., »The Petrarchan Sonneteers and Neo-Platonic Love«, in: *Studies in Philology* 42 (1945) S. 164–182.

Smith, Hallett, »The Sonnets«, in: *Elizabethan Poetry: A Study in Conventions, Meaning, and Expression*, Cambridge (Mass.) 1964 ([1]1952), S. 131–193.

Spiller, Michael R. G., *The Development of the Sonnet: An Intro-*

duction, London 1992. [Zu Wyatt, Surrey, Spenser, Sidney, Shakespeare, Herbert, Milton.]
Weiß, Wolfgang, »Sonette und Sonettsequenzen«, in: W. W., *Die elisabethanische Lyrik*, Darmstadt 1976, S. 68–94. [Zu Wyatt, Surrey, Sidney, Spenser, Shakespeare.]
Wilkins, Ernest H., »The Invention of the Sonnet« (1915, 1959), in: E. H. W., *The Invention of the Sonnet and Other Studies in Italian Literature*, Rom 1959, S. 11–39.

Inhalt

Fremdsprachentexte

IN RECLAMS UNIVERSAL-BIBLIOTHEK

Englische und amerikanische Dramen

Edward Albee: Who's Afraid of Virginia Woolf? 206 S. UB 9073

Samuel Beckett: Waiting for Godot. 147 S. UB 9214

Five English Short Plays. Brenton, Bond, Stoppard, Pinter, Churchill. 210 S. UB 9062

Hanif Kureishi: My Beautiful Laundrette. 166 S. UB 9063

Arthur Miller: The Crucible. 224 S. UB 9257 – Death of a Salesman. 171 S. UB 9172

Marc Norman / Tom Stoppard: Shakespeare in Love. 181 S. UB 9072

Eugene O'Neill: Long Day's Journey into Night. 216 S. UB 9252

J. B. Priestley: An Inspector Calls. 117 S. UB 9218

Willy Russell: Educating Rita. 132 S. UB 9040 – Shirley Valentine. 79 S. UB 9071

Peter Shaffer: Amadeus. 199 S. UB 9219

William Shakespeare: Hamlet. 261 S. UB 9292 – Macbeth. 167 S. UB 9220 – The Merchant of Venice 184 S. UB 9050 – A Midsummer Night's Dream. 160 S. UB 9247 – Romeo and Juliet. 219 S. UB 9005

Bernard Shaw: Mrs Warren's Profession. 198 S. UB 9166 – Pygmalion. 197 S. UB 9266

Tom Stoppard: Rosencrantz and Guildenstern are Dead. 171 S. UB 9185

John Millington Synge: The Playboy of the Western World. 128 S. UB 9211

Oscar Wilde: The Importance of Being Earnest. 141 S. UB 9267 – Lady Windermere's Fan. 101 S. UB 9187

Thornton Wilder: Our Town. 127 S. UB 9168

Tennessee Williams: Cat on a Hot Tin Roof. 224 S. UB 9039 – The Glass Menagerie. 149 S. UB 9178 – A Streetcar Named Desire. 199 S. UB 9240
